THE BASICS OF THE
PERIODIC TABLE

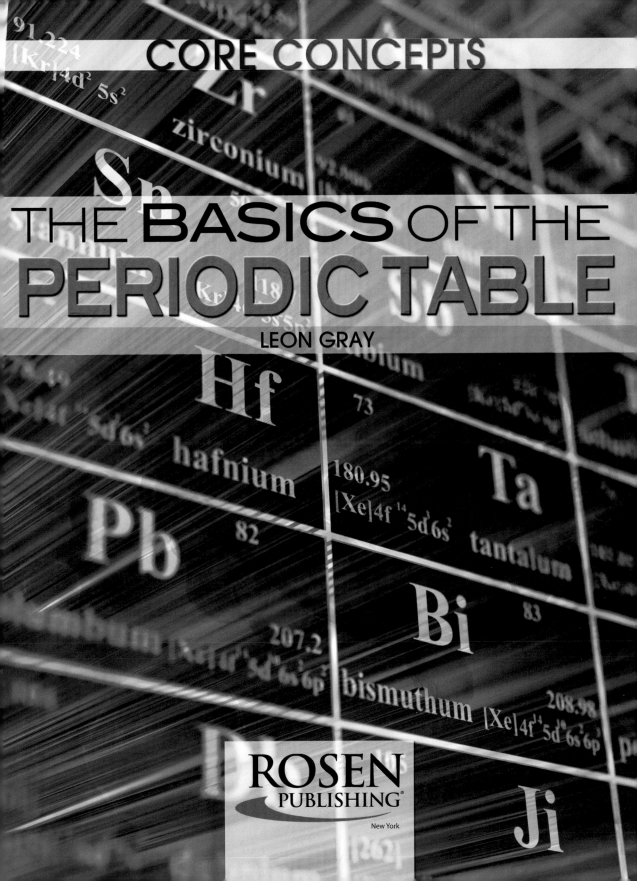

CORE CONCEPTS

THE BASICS OF THE PERIODIC TABLE

LEON GRAY

ROSEN
PUBLISHING®

New York

This edition published in 2014 by:

The Rosen Publishing Group, Inc.
29 East 21st Street
New York, NY 10010

Library of Congress Cataloging-in-Publication Data

Gray, Leon, 1974-
The basics of the periodic table/Leon Gray.—First edition.
      pages cm—(Core concepts)
Includes bibliographical references and index.
ISBN 978-1-4777-2712-6 (library binding)
1. Periodic law—Tables—Juvenile literature. 2. Chemical
elements—Juvenile literature. I. Title.
QD467.G67 2014
546'.8—dc23

                                                          2013024912

Manufactured in the United States of America

CPSIA Compliance Information: Batch #W14YA: For further information, contact Rosen Publishing, New York,
New York, at 1-800-237-9932.

© 2007 Brown Bear Books Ltd.

CONTENTS

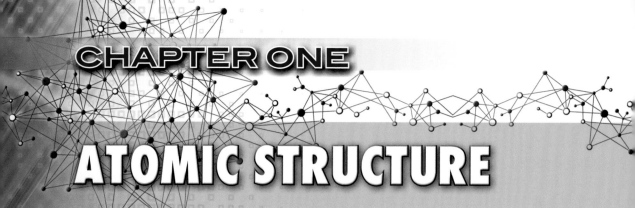

CHAPTER ONE

ATOMIC STRUCTURE

Atoms are the key to how the periodic table is arranged. Each atom has a structure that defines the properties and place in the table of every element.

The periodic table adorns the pages of every chemistry textbook and the walls of every high school laboratory. This simple chart is a "dictionary" for every chemist. It defines the elements, of which everything in the universe is made, in measurable quantities, such as atomic number and atomic mass. It is arranged in a way that highlights similarities between the different elements.

Elements are formed by the stars. As stars burn, they create new elements. When a star explodes as a supernova, these new elements are flung out into space. The red outer ring of this supernova shows the presence of oxygen and neon.

THE BUILDING BLOCKS OF MATTER

The building blocks of matter are called atoms. These tiny particles are so small that scientists can only see them by using powerful microscopes. Almost all atoms consist of even smaller particles called protons, neutrons, and electrons. The protons and neutrons are found in the dense nucleus at the center of the atom. The electrons revolve around the nucleus in a series of layers called electron shells.

A chemical element consists of atoms with the same number of protons in their nucleus. The number of protons is what gives an element its atomic number.

For example, an atom of the element hydrogen (chemical symbol: H) has only 1 proton in its nucleus. An atom of uranium (chemical symbol: U) always has 92 protons in its nucleus. Therefore the atomic number of hydrogen is 1, and the atomic number of uranium is 92.

ELECTRON SHELLS

Each proton has a positive electrical charge. Neutrons have no electrical charge. Each electron has a

The periodic table sets out all the known elements in order of their atomic number. Elements fall into vertical and horizontal families; the members of each family all have similar chemical and physical properties.

negative electrical charge. Atoms are electrically neutral because the number of electrons and protons is the same, so the positive and negative charges cancel out. Thus, a hydrogen atom always has 1 electron, while a uranium atom has 92 electrons.

Electrons revolve around the nucleus in a series of layers, called electron shells, similar to the way in which planets orbit the sun. For this reason, this description of the atom is known as the planetary model.

The electron shells are a series of energy levels, with all the electrons in the same shell having similar energy. An atom can have up to seven shells. Each electron shell can hold only a limited number of electrons. For example, the first shell can hold up to two electrons, the second shell can hold up to eight electrons, the third shell can hold up to 18 electrons, while the fourth shell can hold up to 32 electrons.

IONS

An atom can gain or lose electrons to form what is called an ion. Adding or removing

The Golden Pavilion temple in Kyoto, Japan, built in 1955 as a replacement for the 1397 original, is covered in gold leaf. Gold was one of the elements known to early chemists. Many performed experiments to try to turn other substances into gold, which has always been highly prized.

MOLECULES AND COMPOUNDS

A compound is made up of different elements that are joined by chemical bonds. Water is a compound made of the elements hydrogen and oxygen. Two hydrogen atoms link with one oxygen atom, resulting in one molecule of water. The chemical symbol for hydrogen is H and oxygen is O, but the formula for the water molecule is H2O. This shows that each molecule of water is made from two hydrogen atoms and one oxygen atom.

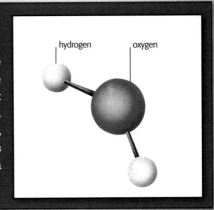

the electrons does not change the atom into the atom of another element. An ion is simply an electrically charged form of the atom. A hydrogen atom may lose its electron to form a hydrogen ion. The hydrogen ion is written as H+. The plus sign means that the hydrogen ion has a positive charge.

It has this positive charge because the negative electron was removed

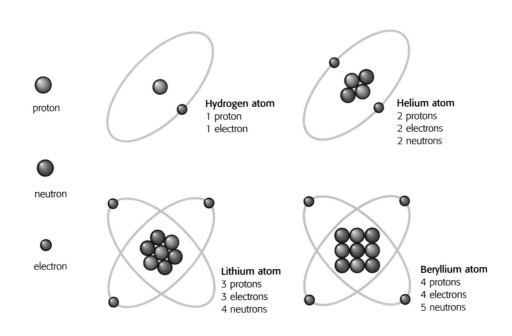

Atoms are made up of protons, electrons, and neutrons. Atoms always have the same number of protons and electrons, but may sometimes have extra neutrons in the nucleus. The first four elements in the periodic table are hydrogen, helium, lithium, and beryllium.

SHELLS AND ORBITALS

The planetary model of the atom came from the pioneering work of scientists in the late 19th and early 20th centuries. However, it soon became clear that atoms were far more complicated. In 1926, Austrian physicist Erwin Schrödinger (1887–1961) came up with the laws of quantum mechanics. In quantum mechanics, electrons are spread around the nucleus in a series of clouds. Each cloud is called an orbital. Orbitals are rather like the electron shells of the planetary model, but the shapes vary with the size of the atom. However, the math used to describe orbitals is complex.

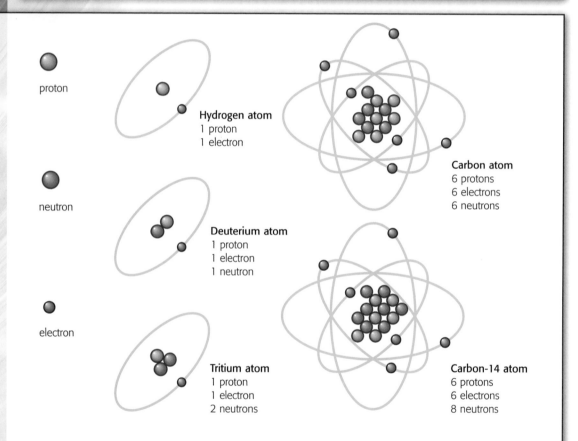

proton

neutron

electron

Hydrogen atom
1 proton
1 electron

Deuterium atom
1 proton
1 electron
1 neutron

Tritium atom
1 proton
1 electron
2 neutrons

Carbon atom
6 protons
6 electrons
6 neutrons

Carbon-14 atom
6 protons
6 electrons
8 neutrons

Many atoms have isotopes, which are versions of the atom that have more than the usual number of neutrons in the nucleus. Hydrogen has two isotopes called deuterium and tritium. Deuterium has one neutron in the nucleus and tritium has two. Carbon usually has six protons and six neutrons in its nucleus, but one of its isotopes has eight neutrons. This isotope is called carbon-14, which indicates the total number of protons and neutrons it contains.

from the atom. This leaves just one positive proton in the atom, resulting in an electrical charge of +1.

STABILIZING THE ATOM

Atoms are stable if the outermost electron shell is full. The atoms of some elements share electrons with the atoms of other elements to make them stable. Other atoms give electrons to the atoms of other elements to become stable. Sharing or transferring electrons results in the formation of a chemical bond between the atoms.

THE SAME BUT DIFFERENT: ISOTOPES

The number of protons is always the same for each element, but the number of neutrons may be different. For example, a carbon atom (chemical symbol: C) always contains six protons in its nucleus. Most carbon atoms contain six neutrons in the nucleus, but some have seven neutrons, and a few have eight neutrons. These different versions of the same element are called isotopes. The number of protons and neutrons in the nucleus of an atom is called the mass number. Most elements are a mixture of different isotopes. Since the

The mineral calcite is a compound made from the elements calcium, oxygen, and carbon. Calcite, or calcium carbonate, is one of the most common minerals on Earth.

KEY TERMS

- **Atomic mass:** The average of all the mass numbers of an element's isotopes.
- **Compound:** A substance made up of a number of different elements joined by chemical bonds.
- **Ion:** An atom that has gained or lost one or more electrons. Atoms that lose electrons form positive ions. Atoms that gain electrons form negative ions.
- **Isotope:** An atom of an element that has a different number of neutrons in its nucleus.
- **Mass number:** The sum of the protons and neutrons in an atom's nucleus.
- **Molecule:** A particle made up of two or more atoms of the same or different elements joined by chemical bonds.

mass number of each isotope is different, scientists take an average of all the mass numbers. The result is the element's official atomic mass.

CHAPTER TWO

DISCOVERING ELEMENTS

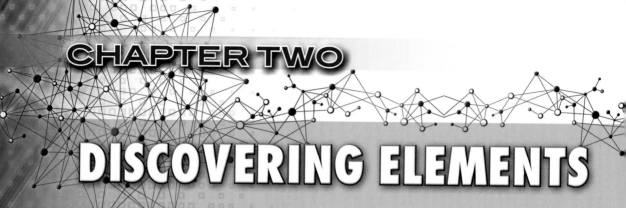

Elements such as gold, mercury, and sulfur have been known for thousands of years, but people did not know that they were elements. Scientists now recognize 118 elements, and there may be more waiting to be discovered.

More than 2,000 years ago, scholars from ancient Greece used the words *atom* and *element* to describe the basic building blocks of matter. Thales of Miletus (c. 625–547 BCE) believed that water was the fundamental substance of which everything in the universe was made. Heracleitus (c. 540–480 BCE) thought that it was fire. Later, Aristotle (384–322 BCE) suggested that everything consisted of a mixture of four different "elements." These were earth, water, air, and fire.

In fact, many elements were already known by the

This image represents the four "elements" of the ancient world: Fireworks represent fire, the river represents water, and earth and air are represented by the land and surrounding air, respectively.

Greek philosopher Aristotle thought that everything was made of only four elements: earth, air, fire, and water.

time of the ancient Greeks. Gold and silver are found as pure elements in nature. These metals were being used from before 5000 BCE. Carbon and sulfur were also known, since they are found as pure elements in nature.

Some metals were vital in the development of human civilization. The Bronze Age, which dates from around 4300 BCE, is a period in history when people mixed copper and tin to make an alloy called bronze. The bronze was then used to make tools and weapons. Iron was first used in present-day Turkey around 1400 BCE, marking the start of the Iron Age. Iron is harder than bronze, so the tools and weapons made from iron were much stronger.

ALCHEMISTS: THE EARLIEST CHEMISTS

New elements started to be discovered from about the 13th century. Early chemists, called alchemists, did many experiments in their search for the philosopher's stone. This mystical substance was thought to turn base metals such as lead into valuable gold and silver. The search for the philosopher's stone was in vain, but alchemists found many important compounds and a few new elements along the way. Among them were antimony (1450) and zinc (1526) and also arsenic, which had been known about since ancient times but was first isolated as an element in 1250.

ELECTROLYSIS

Scientists often use a chemical process called electrolysis to separate elements from their compounds. Electrolysis involves passing electricity through a compound. The compound then splits into positive and negative ions, which move toward a pair of conductors called electrodes. The electrodes are the substances used to conduct the electricity into and out of the compound. Positive ions collect at the negative electrode (cathode), and negative ions collect at the positive electrode (anode). At each electrode, the ions either gain or lose electrons to become atoms again.

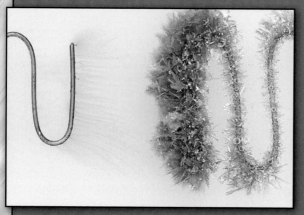

The electrolysis of tin chloride leaves tin on the cathode *(right)* and chlorine gas at the anode *(left)*. This process can be used as a method for plating steel with tin.

German alchemist Hennig Brand (c. 1630–1710) discovered another new element in 1669. He collected his urine in a bottle and concentrated it into a white, glowing solid that he named phosphorus. A few years later, Irish chemist Robert Boyle (1627–1691) read about Brand's experiment. Boyle realized that true elements were substances such as Brand's phosphorus because phosphorus could not be broken down into one of Aristotle's four "elements."

NEW BREAKTHROUGHS

During the 18th century, many scientists did experiments to break down substances into simpler substances. A range of new elements were discovered, such as cobalt, chromium, nickel, and nitrogen. By the end of the 18th century, scientists had identified about 33 elements.

In the early 1800s, English chemist Humphry Davy (1778–1829) found a new way to break down different substances. He passed electricity through compounds to split them up into elements in a process now called electrolysis. In this way, Davy discovered potassium, sodium, calcium, and barium. Other elements were discovered using a technique called spectroscopy, which is the study of objects based on characteristic patterns of light, called spectra, they emit. Using spectroscopy, scientists discovered new elements such as cesium, helium, and xenon.

Two more breakthroughs came before the end of the 19th century. The first was the discovery of the noble gases. Noble gases have full outer electron shells and are largely unreactive, which is why they were not identified for so long. British scientists Lord Rayleigh (1842–1919) and William Ramsay (1852–1916) identified argon in 1894. By 1898, Ramsay had discovered three more noble gases—krypton, neon, and xenon. The second breakthrough came from the work of Polish-born scientist Marie Curie (1867–1934) and her French husband, Pierre Curie (1859–1906). Their studies of radioactivity led to the discovery of radium and polonium in 1898 and helped other scientists identify many more new elements in the 20th century.

Many scientists did important work that helped create the periodic table. Some are given credit for their contribution to modern chemistry, while others have largely been forgotten.

French chemist Antoine-Laurent Lavoisier (1743–1794) made the first

HUMPHRY DAVY

Humphry Davy (1778–1829) was one of the most influential chemists of his time. Born in Penzance, Cornwall, in the United Kingdom, he began his career as an apprentice to an apothecary (an early druggist). In 1799, while he was still a laboratory assistant, Davy discovered the anesthetic effects of laughing gas (nitrous oxide). After he moved to the Royal Institution in 1801, Davy became interested in the new science of electrolysis. Using this method he discovered the elements sodium, potassium, calcium, boron, magnesium, chlorine, strontium, and barium. Davy also speculated that electrolysis worked on a principle of separation by the electrical charge of the element, where positive ions would go to the negative electrode and negative ions to the positive electrode. This theory led to a large-scale expansion of the alkali industry, which made use of the technique.

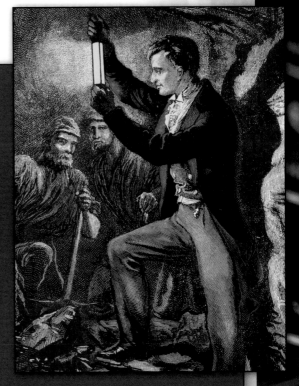

Humphry Davy tests his miner's safety lamp. Prior to this invention, the flame on miners' lamps risked igniting methane in mines. Use of the safety lamp saved the lives of thousands of miners from explosions.

SPECTROSCOPY

Spectroscopy is a technique that is used to identify elements. It works by analyzing the wavelengths of light or other forms of electromagnetic radiation, such as X-rays, microwaves, or radio waves, given off by a substance. All elements give off electromagnetic radiation at specific wavelengths. Many of these wavelengths fall in the range of the visible spectrum, which we see as colors. This effect is best demonstrated by a prism, which splits white light into a rainbow. Each color has its own wavelength and is bent by the prism at a specific angle.

At its simplest, a spectroscope works by collecting the light that is emitted by a substance and passing it through a prism or grating that bends the light into its separate wavelengths. By measuring the angles between the wavelengths and comparing them with a known spectral chart for each element, scientists can determine what the unidentified substance is made from. This technique is very useful in astronomy, where it is used to discover what elements are contained in stars and nebulas.

These colors are the spectrum produced by the element bromine. Each element produces a characteristic spectrum, and this fact enables chemists to discover which elements are present in a sample.

list of elements in his book *Elementary Treatise of Chemistry* (1789). The list included hydrogen, mercury, oxygen, nitrogen, phosphorus, sulfur, and zinc. However, Lavoisier made some mistakes. For example, he put lime on his list of elements. Chemists now know that lime is a compound of calcium and oxygen.

In the early 19th century, British scientist John Dalton (1766–1844) wrote *A New System of Chemical Philosophy*. In his book, Dalton talked about particles called atoms—the building blocks of matter. He suggested that the atoms of different elements had different atomic masses. Different elements then combine in exact amounts to make compounds.

THE TRIADS

German chemist Johann Döbereiner (1780–1849) arranged elements into groups of three, called triads. The members of each triad had similar chemical properties. For example, Döbereiner grouped three soft and reactive metals—lithium, sodium, and potassium. He also grouped three pungent and harmful elements: chlorine, bromine, and iodine. As well as having similar chemical properties, the atomic mass of the middle element in each triad was the average of the other two elements. Döbereiner published his "law of triads" in 1829.

By 1843, German chemist Leopold Gmelin (1788–1853) added elements to Döbereiner's triads. Gmelin added fluorine to the triad of chlorine, bromine, and iodine, making one group of four, called a tetrad. Gmelin recognized that oxygen, sulfur, selenium, and tellurium had similar chemical properties, so he grouped them together.

THE TELLURIC SPIRAL

In 1860, Italian chemist Stanislao Cannizzaro (1826–1910) published a list of the atomic masses of the known

ELEMENTS.

		w.t			w.t
	Hydrogen.	1		Strontian	46
	Azote	5		Barytes	68
	Carbon	5		Iron	50
	Oxygen	7		Zinc	56
	Phosphorus	9		Copper	56
	Sulphur	13		Lead	90
	Magnesia	20		Silver	190
	Lime	24		Gold	190
	Soda	28		Platina	190
	Potash	42		Mercury	167

In 1808, John Dalton produced a list of elements and their atomic mass and gave each element a circular symbol.

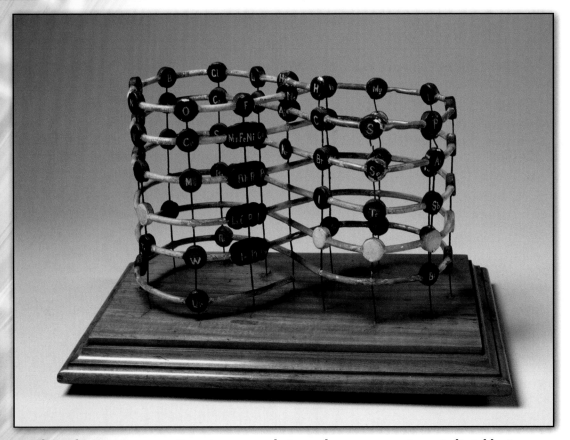

In the 19th century, many attempts were made to produce an accurate periodic table. In 1888, English scientist William Crookes produced this spiral periodic table.

elements. The list was announced at a science meeting in Karlsruhe, Germany.

Many scientists attended the meeting. Among them was a geology professor from France, Alexandre-Emile Bèguyer de Chancourtois (1820–1886). De Chancourtois came up with one of the earliest periodic tables. He arranged the known elements in order of atomic mass. De Chancourtois placed the elements in a spiral around a cylinder. He noticed that Gmelin's tetrad—oxygen, sulfur, selenium, and tellurium—formed a vertical column on the spiral. De Chancourtois called his arrangement of elements the "telluric spiral" because tellurium fell in the center of the spiral.

NEWLANDS'S LAW OF OCTAVES

In 1864, English chemist John Alexander Reina Newlands (1837–1898) listed the known elements in order of increasing atomic mass. He found that an element in this order shared its chemistry with

JOHN NEWLANDS

John Alexander Reina Newlands was born in London, England, on November 26, 1837. His father was a religious minister from Scotland, and his mother's family came from Italy. Newlands studied under his father at home and then attended the Royal College of Chemistry in 1856. Later, he worked as an industrial chemist.

When Newlands came up with his "law of octaves," his fellow scientists dismissed the work as nonsense. When the periodic table eventually became accepted, scientists realized that Newlands's law was right. Newlands eventually got the recognition he deserved in the form of a Royal Society Davy Medal in 1882. He died of influenza in 1898.

elements eight places before and after it. He called this pattern his law of octaves because it was like the eight musical notes in an octave. Newlands announced his law of octaves in 1866, but chemists did not treat his discovery seriously.

ODLING'S TABLE IS IGNORED

The year 1864 was a busy time for chemists trying to organize the elements. First,

KEY TERMS

- **Atomic mass:** The sum of the number of protons and neutrons in an atom's nucleus.
- **Electrolysis:** A chemical reaction caused by passing an electric current through a liquid.
- **Four elements:** In ancient times, people believed that everything in the universe was made of four elements: earth, air, fire, and water.

English chemist William Odling (1829–1921), president of the Chemical Society of London, published a chart of known elements in order of atomic mass. Odling did not organize all the known elements, and he left gaps to suggest some unknown elements. Like Newlands's table, Odling's table was ignored, but is no less important. In the same year, German chemist Julius Lothar Meyer (1830–1895) published a table of about 49 elements. In his table, Meyer listed the elements by valence. Valence is the usual number of bonds an atom can form with other atoms. Eventually, Meyer revised the list in order of atomic mass, but with elements of similar valence grouped in columns. Meyer had created the first periodic table, but he took too long to publish his findings. A young Russian chemist named Dmitri Ivanovich Mendeleev beat him to it.

CHAPTER THREE

DEVISING THE MODERN PERIODIC TABLE

The modern periodic table was devised by Russian chemist Dmitri Ivanovich Mendeleev (1834–1907). New elements have since been added, but the basic structure of Mendeleev's table remains the same.

Legend has it that Mendeleev came up with the periodic table when he was playing a card game called solitaire. There is little historical evidence, however, to back up this account. It is clear that Mendeleev arranged the table using a list of atomic masses produced in 1860 at a science meeting in Karlsruhe, Germany. Atomic mass is the sum of the number of protons and neutrons in an atom's nucleus. Mendeleev believed that atomic mass was the most important property of an element, though we now know that elements are defined by

Lightbulbs typically contain the noble gas argon. The noble gases rarely react with other elements and so were the last group of elements to be discovered and the last group to be added to the periodic table.

Dmitri Ivanovich Mendeleev was one of the most influential scientists of his time. His periodic table revolutionized chemistry and helped scientists discover new elements.

writing a textbook, *The Principles of Chemistry* (1868–1870). In this book, Mendeleev grouped elements with similar physical and chemical properties. For example, he grouped the halogens (Group 17 elements) in one chapter and the alkali metals in another chapter.

Mendeleev was grouping elements with the same valence. Valence is a measure of the number of bonds an atom can form with other atoms. Valence is determined by the number of electrons in the outer electron shell of an atom. Atoms share or transfer these outer electrons, forming chemical bonds with other atoms. The halogens have similar properties because they all have seven electrons

their atomic number—the number of protons in an atom's nucleus.

It is likely that Mendeleev came up with the periodic table while he was

DMITRI MENDELEEV

Dmitri Ivanovich Mendeleev was born in Tobol'sk, Siberia, on February 8, 1834. From an early age, it was clear that he was a talented scientist. His mother tried to find him a place at a university, but Mendeleev was turned away from the Russian universities of Moscow and St. Petersburg. Finally, in 1850, he enrolled as a trainee science teacher at the Institute of St. Petersburg and graduated with distinction. In 1855, he took a job as a science teacher at Simferopol near the Black Sea. A year later, he returned to St. Petersburg and completed a master's degree.

In 1859, he traveled abroad to work in laboratories in Europe. On his return in 1861, Mendeleev focused on an academic career and eventually became a chemistry professor at St. Petersburg University. In 1869, he published his first version of the periodic table. His final years were spent as director of the Bureau of Weights and Measures in St. Petersburg. Mendeleev received many awards from universities around the world. In 1906, he came within one vote of receiving the Nobel Prize in Chemistry. He died in St. Petersburg in 1907.

Scientists think that the blue color in aquamarine gemstones is caused by small quantities of scandium. Before scandium was discovered, Mendeleev predicted its existence using his periodic table.

they all readily donate the electron to form bonds with other elements.

As Mendeleev tried to group similar elements, a pattern emerged. He arranged the 61 known elements in a chart in order of increasing atomic mass. Mendeleev found that elements with the same valence appeared in the same columns of the chart. Mendeleev had outlined the basic structure of the periodic table. He published his findings in 1869 and produced a revised table in 1871 that placed the elements into eight groups.

in the outer electron shell, and they all readily accept one electron to form bonds with other elements. In contrast, the alkali metals share physical and chemical properties because they have just one electron in the outer electron shell, and

DESCRIBING UNDISCOVERED ELEMENTS

One of Mendeleev's great achievements was to move elements to new places in the chart despite upsetting the order suggested by atomic mass. In this way, he kept the order of elements by valence. Perhaps the greatest achievement, however, was to describe elements that had not yet been discovered. Mendeleev was convinced of the natural order of the periodic table. His table, however, contained gaps, and Mendeleev reasoned that these gaps must represent elements not yet discovered. He even predicted the physical and chemical properties of these missing elements.

WHAT'S IN A NAME?

There is no right or wrong way to spell Mendeleev's name in English. In Russian, words are written using the Cyrillic alphabet, for which there is no literal English translation. Consequently, you might see Mendeleev's name written as Mendeev, Mendeleyev, Mendeleeff, or Mendelaev.

Arc welding uses an electric current to produce a sparklike electric arc that fuses metals together by melting them. Argon is sometimes used in arc welding because it is an inert gas, so it does not react with the molten metal, resulting in a more stable arc.

One of these gaps occurred below aluminum in Mendeleev's table, so he named it eka-aluminum (*eka* is Sanskrit for "one," and eka-aluminum is one place from aluminum in the periodic table). This element was discovered by French scientist Paul-Emile Lecoq de Boisbaudran (1838–1912) in 1875. He called it gallium in honor of his country (Gallia is the Latin name for France). In 1879, Swedish chemist Lars Frederick Nilson (1840–1899) discovered the element that Mendeleev called eka-boron. Nilson named this element scandium in honor of Scandinavia. In 1886, German chemist Clemens Winkler (1838–1904) discovered Mendeleev's eka-silicon. Winkler named it germanium in honor of Germany. In all cases, the properties of the new elements matched Mendeleev's predictions.

THE NOBLE GASES

In 1895, English chemist John William Strutt, later known as Lord Rayleigh (1842–1919), and Scottish chemist William Ramsay (1852–1916) identified

William Ramsay won the Nobel Prize for chemistry in 1904 for his work on the discovery of the noble gases.

Travers. Together, they identified neon, krypton, and xenon. Four years later, Mendeleev revised his periodic table. He put the new group of gases in a group at the end of the periodic table. Chemists originally named this family of elements "inert gases" because they could not be made to react with other elements. Inert gases are now called noble gases because they do react in certain circumstances.

ARRANGING ELEMENTS BY ATOMIC NUMBER

In 1911, New Zealand–born British physicist Ernest Rutherford (1871–1937) carried out an important experiment. This experiment revealed that the center of an atom consists of a dense, positively charged nucleus. Two years after Rutherford's discovery, English physicist Henry Moseley (1887–1915) used a machine called an electron gun to fire electrons at the atoms of different elements. He found

a gas that they called argon. The new element did not seem to fit anywhere in Mendeleev's periodic table. Ramsay thought that similar gases to argon must exist, and so he set about trying to find them. In 1895, he produced helium. In 1898, he carried out further research with English chemist Morris

KEY TERMS

- Atomic mass: The number of protons and neutrons in a nucleus.
- Atomic number: The number of protons in an atom's nucleus.
- Noble gases: A group of gases that rarely react with other elements.
- Valence: A measure of the number of bonds an atom can form with other atoms.

that the elements gave off X-rays—high-energy radiation with short wavelengths. These X-rays had characteristics that depended on the number of protons in the nucleus. Moseley wrote down the proton number (now called atomic number) of many different elements. He then made a chart of all the known elements in order of increasing proton number. Following in Mendeleev's footsteps, Moseley also left gaps in his chart, predicting the existence of two new elements.

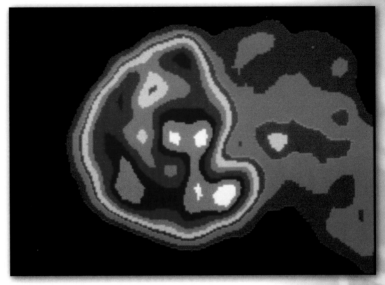

An isotope of technetium is commonly used in some scans that enable doctors to see inside a patient's body. This scan shows a brain in profile.

These missing elements were later discovered and are called technetium and promethium. Moseley also corrected some of the errors associated with a table arranged by atomic mass.

ATOMIC NUMBER VS. ATOMIC MASS

Atomic mass is a measure of the number of protons and neutrons in the nucleus of an atom. The atoms of an element always contain the same number of protons, but they may have different numbers of neutrons. These different versions of atoms are called isotopes. Atomic number is the basic property on which the periodic table is best organized, not atomic mass. Fortunately for Mendeleev, who did not know about protons and neutrons, atomic mass and atomic number increase roughly in proportion.

FINAL ARRANGEMENTS

The last major change to the periodic table came in the middle of the 20th century. American physicist Glenn Seaborg (1912–1999) and his colleagues discovered 11 new elements with atomic numbers greater than that of uranium (atomic number 92). Seaborg rearranged the periodic table to accommodate these new elements.

CHAPTER FOUR

HOW TO READ THE PERIODIC TABLE

The periodic table organizes all the chemical elements into a simple chart according to the physical and chemical properties of their atoms

The periodic table arranges elements in order of increasing atomic number. The rows are called periods and the columns are called groups. In general, elements in the same column have similar chemical properties. The arrangement of the electrons in the atoms of elements determines the structure of the periodic table itself.

THE ORDER OF THE ELEMENTS

The atomic number of an element is the number of protons in the nucleus of one atom of that element. A hydrogen atom always has one proton in its nucleus. The atomic number is 1, so hydrogen takes first place in the periodic table. A helium atom always has two protons in the nucleus. Its atomic number is 2, so it is second in the table, after hydrogen. A uranium atom always has 92 protons in its nucleus. The atomic number is 92, so uranium takes 92nd position.

Arranging elements in order of their atomic number eliminates the problems Mendeleev had when he organized the elements in order of atomic mass. From left to right along a row of the periodic table, the atomic number rises by one whole unit for each element. Elements in lower rows have higher atomic numbers than elements above. Chemists can be absolutely sure that there are no missing atomic numbers and no missing elements.

WHAT'S IN THE BOX?

Each box of the periodic table represents one element. The box must show the element's atomic number, its name, and its chemical symbol. Aside from this, there are no strict rules. The atomic mass of the element is usually included,

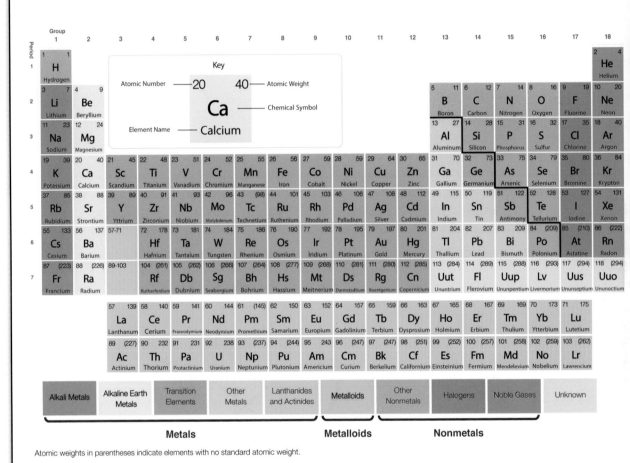

The classic representation of the periodic table sets the elements out into 18 groups arranged in 7 rows. Rows are arranged in order of increasing atomic number, from left to right. All the members of a group show related properties in the way they react chemically with other groups in the table. All the gases except hydrogen are at the upper right of the table, and the metals are all in the left and center. Metals constitute the bulk of the elements. Most of the radioactive elements are in the actinide group.

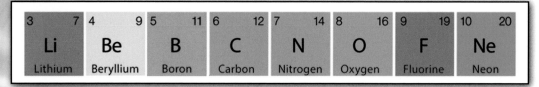

3	7	4	9	5	11	6	12	7	14	8	16	9	19	10	20
Li		**Be**		**B**		**C**		**N**		**O**		**F**		**Ne**	
Lithium		Beryllium		Boron		Carbon		Nitrogen		Oxygen		Fluorine		Neon	

Period 2 of the periodic table begins with lithium and ends with neon. As the elements progress along the row, their chemical nature changes from metallic (Li and Be) to metalloid (B), to nonmetallic (C), and finally gaseous (N, O, F, and Ne).

since it reflects the history of the periodic table. Some versions may have up to 20 data sets for each element, including, for example, electron arrangements and whether the element is normally a solid, liquid, or gas at standard conditions of temperature and pressure. In many modern tables, the elements are also shaded according to type, showing which are metals, nonmetals, and metalloids. Other tables have individual shading for specific groups of elements, for example, one color for the alkali metals, one for the alkaline earths, one for the halogens, and so on. Not all are arranged in straight rows or

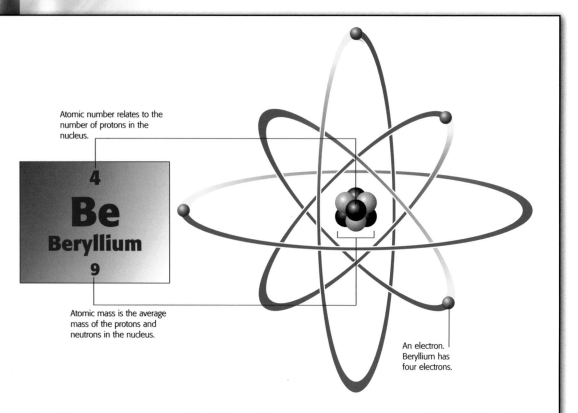

Atomic number relates to the number of protons in the nucleus.

4

Be

Beryllium

9

Atomic mass is the average mass of the protons and neutrons in the nucleus.

An electron. Beryllium has four electrons.

How the atomic structure of beryllium relates to its representation in the periodic table.

PERIODS

The seven main rows of the periodic table are called periods. Hydrogen and helium make up Period 1. Next come the two short periods of eight elements: Period 2 starts with lithium (atomic number 3) and ends with neon (10). Period 3 starts with sodium (11) and ends with argon (18). Then come the two long periods, each of 18 elements. Period 4 starts with potassium (19) and ends on krypton (36). Period 5 starts with rubidium (37) and ends with xenon (54). Some of the elements in the long periods 4 and 5 are called transition metals. In Period 4, the transition metals start with scandium (21) and end with zinc (30). In Period 5, the transition metals start with yttrium (39) and end with cadmium (48).

Period 6 is a very long row of 32 elements, starting with cesium (55) and ending with radon (86). In most modern periodic tables, Period 6 is reduced to 18 elements by moving 14 elements, called the lanthanides, to the bottom of the table. Not only does the table then fit on a normal size page, it also allows elements with similar valence to be placed in the same columns. (Valence depends on the number of electrons in the outer shell and determines the reactivity of the element.) So the transition metals in Period 6 end with mercury (80),

One of the chief sources of the element beryllium is a mineral made up of aluminum, silicon, and oxygen. One of its crystalline forms is aquamarine, which is cut into a sparkling pale blue gemstone. Emerald is another form of this mineral.

columns. Some are arranged in spirals or in shapes that represent relationships between the elements' chemical properties.

Plants and animals rely on three of the Period 2 elements to live and grow. Carbon and the gases nitrogen and oxygen make up about 90 percent of the dry weight of all living organisms.

which lies directly below cadmium, the last transition metal in Period 5.

Period 7 begins with Francium and ends with the artificial element 118 (temporarily named ununoctium, which is Latin for 118). Artificial elements do not occur in nature but have been created in laboratories by scientists. Period 7 is another very long period of 32 elements that was completed when element 118 was discovered in 2006. Period 7 is also shortened by moving 14 elements, called the actinides, to the bottom of the table.

GROUPS

Elements with the same number of electrons in their outer electron shells are usually found in columns called groups. Chemists place hydrogen at the top of Group 1, but it is not really part of the group. Group 1 actually starts with lithium (3) and ends with francium (87). Unlike hydrogen, the Group 1 elements are soft, strong, metals. All of them react with water to form alkaline solutions. For this reason, the Group 1 elements are called the alkali metals.

The Group 2 elements start with beryllium (4) and end with radium (88). The Group 2 elements are known as the alkaline-earth metals. These metals also react with water to form alkaline solutions. The word *earth* comes from an old term used to describe the compounds formed when the Group 2 metals reacted with oxygen.

Groups 3 to 12 comprise the transition metals in the center of the periodic table and rare-earth metals at the bottom of the table. The chemistry of the transition metals is less predictable than that of the alkali and alkaline-earth metals. Some transition metals, such as cobalt (27) and iron (26), form many different colored compounds.

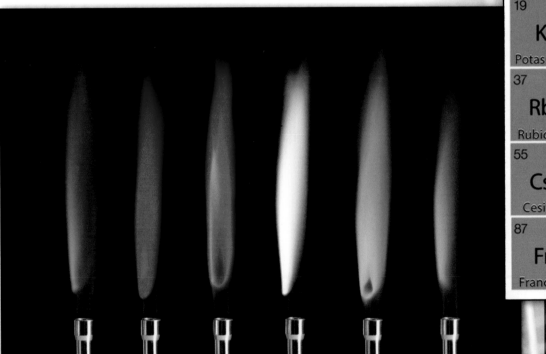

1	1
H	
Hydrogen	
3	7
Li	
Lithium	
11	23
Na	
Sodium	
19	39
K	
Potassium	
37	85
Rb	
Rubidium	
55	133
Cs	
Cesium	
87	(223)
Fr	
Francium	

Flame tests, where a sample is burned in a flame, can be used to identify elements. This series shows metal elements, including copper, lithium, strontium, sodium, copper (again), and potassium.

A HOME FOR HYDROGEN

In most versions of the periodic table, hydrogen is put above the alkali metals in Group 1 at the top left of the periodic table. There is a problem with this, however, because hydrogen is a gas and all the Group 1 elements are metals. In other versions of the table, hydrogen can be found above the halogens in Group 17. Sometimes, hydrogen appears in both groups, and sometimes it is left to float freely at the top of the table. In fact, hydrogen is a unique element that no one really knows where to place.

Others, such as gold (79) and platinum (78), hardly react at all and can be found as pure metals in nature.

Groups 13, 14, 15, and 16 form groups of elements that do not seem as clearly related as the previous groups. Metalloids (metal-like elements), such as boron (6) and silicon (14), and many solid nonmetals, such as phosphorus (15) and sulfur (16), are found in groups 13 through 16. The halogens make up Group 17. This group starts with fluorine (9) and ends with ununseptium (117). All halogens are reactive, and fluorine is the most reactive of all the elements.

Transition metals form compounds of many colors. That makes them very useful in the glass industry, where this property helps make colored marbles.

CHEMICAL SYMBOLS

A chemical symbol is the shorthand way of writing an element's name. Chemical symbols are used in writing chemical equations. The symbol itself consists of either one or two letters. Usually, the symbol is the first letter of the element's common name. So, hydrogen is "H," and boron is "B." Sometimes the symbol is the first letter of the element's Latin name. For example, potassium is "K," after its Latin name *kalium*. Inevitably, the names of some elements start with the same letter, so a symbol may consist of two letters. Only the first letter is a capital. So, helium is "He," while barium is "Ba." Iron has the chemical symbol Fe for its Latin name *ferrum*.

The Group 18 elements start with helium (2) and end with ununoctium (118). These gases had not been discovered when Mendeleev's original table was published in 1869. Mendeleev added them to the end of his revised table in 1902. The Group 18 elements do not react with many other elements. For this reason, they are known as the noble, or inert, gases.

NUMBERING SYSTEMS

From the top to the bottom of the periodic table, the periods (rows) are simply numbered 1 through 7. The numbering

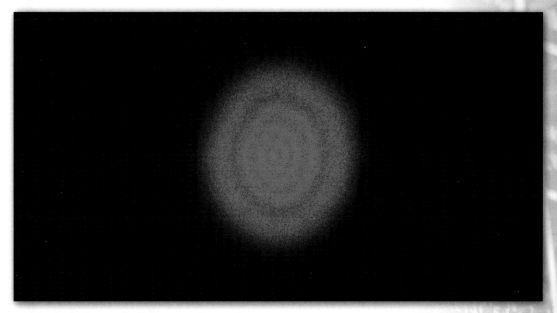

The light from a helium-neon laser shines on an aperture, creating diffraction. Helium and neon are the first two elements in the noble gases, which comprise the Group 18 elements.

AN ELEMENT BY ANY OTHER NAME

Deciding what to call an element has posed a challenge to scientists throughout the centuries. Of the elements that have been known longest, most countries have their own names for elements such as gold, silver, or mercury. For example, France and Greece call nitrogen *azote*, and Germany uses *Sauerstoff* for oxygen. Some use versions of the Latin names and are very similar. Silver is *argentum* in Latin, which is changed to *argento* in Italian and *argent* in French.

To avoid confusion in international trade and ensure that scientists of all nations can talk about the same element without any risk of misidentification, element names have been standardized. The body that oversees this process is the International Union of Pure and Applied Chemistry, or IUPAC. Among its rulings are that, internationally, aluminum and cesium should be known by their British spellings "aluminium" and "caesium" but that sulfur should take the U.S. spelling (not sulphur).

With new elements still being synthesized in the laboratory, IUPAC is also involved in the naming process. Often the new element has been found by two or more laboratories and they may have different ideas about what to call it. There have been many arguments over what to call the heavy elements with atomic numbers between 104 and 111. These have now been agreed as rutherfordium (104), dubnium (105), seaborgium (106), bohrium (107), hassium (108), meitnerium (109), darmstadtium (110), and roentgenium (111). Some elements beyond these are known by a Latinized form of their atomic number—ununtrium (113), ununpentium (115), ununseptium (117), and ununoctium (118).

Most of the elements are named after places or people. The places are usually where the element was first discovered or the discoverer's country. Those named after people honor famous scientists or characters from mythology. A few are named after astronomical objects.

Helios, the Greek sun god after whom helium is named.

ELEMENTS NAMED AFTER PLACES

Americium—the Americas
Californium—the state of California
Darmstadtium—Darmstadt, Germany
Europium—Europe
Francium—France
Hafnium—Hafnia, Latin for Copenhagen
Holmium—Holmia, Latin for Stockholm
Lutetium—Lutetia, Latin for Paris
Magnesium—Magnesia, Greece
Polonium—Poland
Strontium—Strontian, Scotland
Ytterbium, Yttrium—Ytterby, Sweden

ELEMENTS NAMED AFTER PEOPLE OR GODS

Bohrium—Niels Bohr
Curium—Pierre and Marie Curie
Einsteinium—Albert Einstein
Fermium—Enrico Fermi
Helium—Helios, the Greek sun god
Mendelevium—Dmitri Mendeleev
Niobium—Niobe, a woman in Greek mythology
Nobelium—Alfred Nobel
Selenium—Selene, Greek goddess of the moon
Thorium—Thor, the Scandinavian god of thunder
Tellurium—Tellus, Latin name for Earth
Vanadium—Vanadis, a Scandinavian goddess

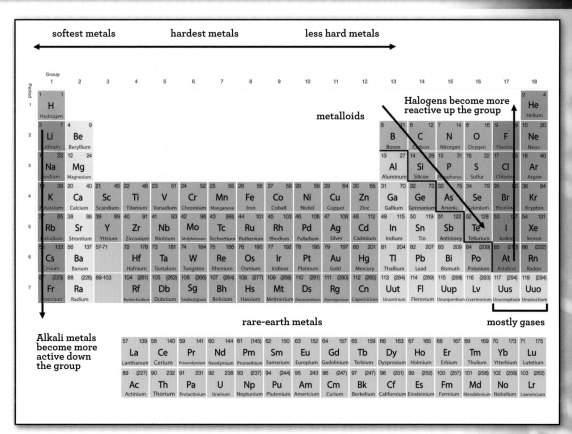

Arranging the elements in the periodic table reveals certain trends across periods and up and down groups, such as hardness, reactivity, and physical state.

MELTING AND BOILING POINTS ACROSS PERIOD 2

		Element							
		Lithium	**Beryllium**	**Boron**	**Carbon**	**Nitrogen**	**Oxygen**	**Fluorine**	**Neon**
melting point	°F	357	2,349	3,769	6,381	−346	−361	−363	−415
	°C	180.5	1,287	2,076	3,527	−210	−218	−219	−248
boiling point	°F	2,448	4,476	7,101	7,281	−320	−297	−306	−411
	°C	1,342	2,469	3,927	4,027	−196	−183	−188	−246

Uranium is one of the rare-earth elements. It is sometimes added to glass to give it a luminous yellow color.

numbers (I, II, III, IV, V, and so on). The second system uses a combination of Roman numbers and the letters A and B. In 1985, the International Union of Pure and Applied Chemistry (IUPAC) replaced the traditional Roman numbers and letters. The new system uses the Arabic numbers 1 to 18, starting with the alkali metals (Group 1) and ending with the noble gases (Group 18). You may still see the traditional system used in modern textbooks because many chemists did not want to change the Roman number convention.

TREND-SPOTTING

Today, the periodic table consists of 118 elements in seven periods and 18 groups. At standard conditions (room temperature and pressure), two of these elements are liquids (bromine and mercury), 11 are gases, and the rest are solids. Aside from hydrogen and mercury, the gases and liquids are on the right of the

of the groups is more problematic. There are three systems for numbering the groups. The first uses Roman

COLOR IN THE PERIODIC TABLE

Search for a few different versions of the periodic table on the Internet. Compare them to the one printed in this book. Which table do you think works best? Use a printer to make some copies of the periodic tables you have found.

You could also take a photocopy of the periodic table in this book. Then shade in one color all the elements that are metals. Then shade in all the gases in another color. Shade the remaining boxes that are neither metals nor gases using a different color. You might need to do some research before you start coloring in the boxes to find out which elements are metals, which are gases, and which are neither.

RARE-EARTH METALS

In most versions of the periodic table, two rows of 14 elements can be found at the bottom of the table. The 14 elements in the first row are called the lanthanide elements, and those in the second row are called the actinide elements. The reason for the separation is a practical one. A period with the full complement of 32 elements is simply too long to fit on a normal page. However, most chemists agree that the chemistry of the lanthanides and actinides is similar enough for the elements to form a separate group, called the rare-earth metals.

KEY TERMS

- Boiling point: The temperature at which a liquid turns into a gas.
- Melting point: The temperature at which a solid turns into a liquid.
- Standard conditions: Normal room temperature and pressure.

table. Most metals are on the left-hand side and bottom of the table. The metalloids form a diagonal line, from boron to tellurium, on the right-hand side of the table. Most nonmetals, such as carbon, oxygen, nitrogen, and the halogens, are on the right and top of the table (aside from the noble gases). Thus there is a general trend for elements to become less metal-like from left to right across a period.

The alkali metals in Group 1 are soft metals with low melting points. The alkaline-earth metals in Group 2 are harder and have higher melting points than the metals of Group 1. Moving from left to right across the periods, elements gradually get harder and have higher melting and boiling points. These properties peak at the center of the table. The hardness, melting, and boiling points then begin to fall again.

CHAPTER FIVE

THE MIGHTY METALS

About three-quarters of all the elements are metals. In general, metals are found on the left and in the middle of the periodic table. Some metals, such as gold and copper, were among the first elements to have been discovered.

In nature, most metals are found mixed with other elements in rocks, forming compounds called ores. The ores of the metals are usually compounds of oxygen (oxides) or sulfur (sulfides). A few metals, such as gold, platinum, and silver, occur naturally as pure metals.

Metals such as aluminum, copper, iron, and magnesium have many properties such as hardness and strength that make them useful elements. As a result, many metal ores are mined. The metals are then extracted from their ores in a process called refining.

LOCATING THE METALS

Different metals are found in different parts of the table. The alkali metals (Group 1) and alkaline-earth metals (Group 2) can be found on the left side of the table. The transition metals (groups 3–12) are located in the middle of the table. Aluminum

Cog wheels in mechanical devices are commonly made of metals. Many metals are hard and strong, making them ideal for objects that need to withstand a lot of wear and tear.

(Group 13) and lead and tin (Group 14) are found toward the right side of the table. The rare-earth metals form two rows underneath the main body of the table. The rare-earth metals are considered in chapter 8 of this book.

PHYSICAL CHARACTERISTICS

There are so many different metals that it is hard to talk about general properties. Most metals are hard, dense, and strong solids at room temperature. Mercury is the only metal that is liquid at room temperature. Some metals, such as sodium and lithium, are also soft at room temperature and can be cut with a knife. Most metals are silver or gray, but copper is brownish orange and gold is yellow. The surface of a metal shines (has a luster) when it is polished. Most but not all metals have high melting points. The melting point is the

temperature at which a solid turns into a liquid. Tungsten has the highest melting point of all the metals—6,192 degrees Fahrenheit (3,422°C). Gallium, however, melts if you hold a piece in your hands. Most metals also have high boiling points. The boiling point is the temperature at which a liquid turns into a gas.

Metals are malleable, which means they can be beaten into different shapes. One ounce (28 g) of gold can be beaten into a sheet 100 feet square (9.3 m²). Metals are also ductile, which means they can be drawn into fine wires. A thread

The metals form the largest group in the periodic table. They are broadly divided into transition metals (Groups 3–12), alkali metals (Group 1), and alkaline-earth metals (Group 2). There are also some metals that fall into Groups 13, 14, 15, and 16.

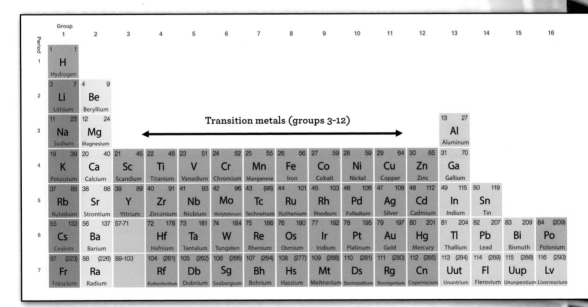

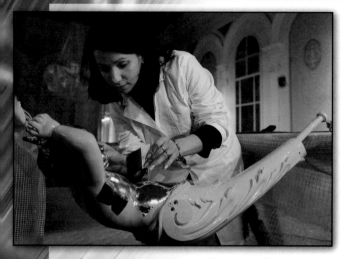

This restoration specialist is applying gold leaf to a chandelier as a decorative coating. Sheets of gold leaf are only 4–5 millionths of an inch (10–12.4 millionths of a centimeter) thick.

CRYSTAL LATTICES

In a face-centered cubic lattice, the atoms form a cube with a single atom in the center of each face.

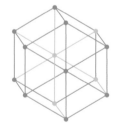

In a hexagonal lattice, the atoms form the shape of a hexagon.

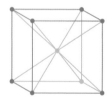

In a body-centered cubic lattice, the atoms form a cube with a single atom at the center of the cube.

drawn from 1 ton (0.907 metric ton) of gold would stretch to the Moon and back. Most metals are also elastic substances. You can stretch and bend a piece of metal and it will return to its original shape. Metals are also good conductors of heat and electricity.

METALLIC STRUCTURE

Metals are crystalline structures. A solid piece of metal is a huge network of neatly arranged atoms in the form of crystals. This is called a giant lattice structure. The atoms of the metal pack tightly to form the crystals, which are shaped like cubes or hexagons. The bonds holding the atoms together are rigid, making the metal very strong. The tight packing of the atoms makes most metals heavy and dense. Density is a measure of the mass of a substance per unit volume. Osmium and iridium have the highest densities of all the elements.

Sometimes there are defects in the crystal structure. When there is a defect, the atoms in the crystals slide over each other. This makes the metal easy to stretch and bend and easy to beat into different shapes. That explains why most metals are ductile and malleable. However, too many defects in the crystal make the metal brittle.

KEY TERMS

- **Ductile:** Ductile materials can be stretched easily.
- **Malleable:** Malleable materials can be easily worked into different shapes.
- **Ore:** Rock that contains useful elements such as aluminum, copper, iron, or platinum.
- **Refining:** An industrial process that frees elements, such as metals, from impurities or unwanted material.

In the atoms of most metals, the electrons in the outer electron shell are not held tightly within the atom. Some of the electrons break free and move among the metal atoms.

A metal is therefore a mass of positive ions—metal atoms that have lost electrons. The metal ions are surrounded by a "sea" of electrons. Dutch physicist Hendrik Lorentz (1853–1928) came up with this model of the structure of metals in the early 20th century. It explains why most metals are good conductors. Electricity flows when all the electrons in the sea move in a particular direction.

THE REACTIVITY OF METALS

The atoms of most metals readily give up their outer electrons to the atoms of other elements. Metals therefore form positive ions when they react with other elements, typically nonmetals. The nonmetal atoms accept the electrons and become negative ions. Some metals are much more reactive than others. Potassium and sodium are highly reactive metals. These metals react strongly with water and violently with acids. In both cases, the reaction produces a lot of hydrogen gas and heat. However, gold and silver hardly react at all, even when concentrated (strong)

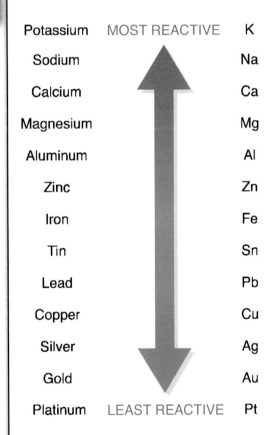

REACTIVITY SERIES

Potassium	MOST REACTIVE	K
Sodium		Na
Calcium		Ca
Magnesium		Mg
Aluminum		Al
Zinc		Zn
Iron		Fe
Tin		Sn
Lead		Pb
Copper		Cu
Silver		Ag
Gold		Au
Platinum	LEAST REACTIVE	Pt

This diagram shows the reactivity series for a selection of metals. Reactivity is a measure of a metal's tendency to react. The most reactive metals are those in Group 1, represented here by potassium and sodium.

acids are poured on them. The reactivity series is a list of metals in order of their reactivity. Metals at the top of the series are the most reactive.

So the Group 1 metals are found at the top of the reactivity series, and metals such as gold and silver are found at the bottom of the table.

GROUP 1: THE ALKALI METALS

The alkali metals form Group 1 of the periodic table. They are lithium, sodium, potassium, rubidium, cesium, and francium. The alkali metals are not very dense. Sodium and potassium are soft enough to be cut with a knife. All the alkali metals have just one electron in their outer electron shell. When they react with other elements, alkali metals lose this outer electron. The metal becomes a positive ion with a stable arrangement of electrons. The alkali metals therefore form ionic compounds with other elements, particularly the halogens. The alkali metals are the most reactive of all the metals. Common compounds of alkali metals include sodium chloride (table salt) and potassium chloride (a fertilizer).

A piece of magnesium ribbon burns with a brilliant white light in air. Magnesium is used in flares, aircraft parts, and fireworks.

GROUP 2: THE ALKALINE-EARTH METALS

The alkaline earths form Group 2 of the periodic table. They are beryllium,

METALS IN THE BODY

Some metals are vital to body processes. For example, a substance called hemoglobin in the blood contains iron. Hemoglobin enables the blood to carry oxygen from the lungs around the body. Calcium and potassium are needed to transmit signals along nerve cells. Calcium also makes bones and teeth strong and hard. Magnesium plays a role in controlling heartbeat and the functioning of muscles.

magnesium, calcium, strontium, barium, and radium. Like the alkali metals, the alkaline earths are not as hard or as dense as most other metals. Alkaline-earth metals have two electrons in their outer electron shell. Like the alkali metals, the alkaline earths form ionic compounds with other elements. These metals donate their two outer electrons, forming ions with an electrical charge of +2. The ions formed have an extremely stable arrangement of electrons.

Calcium is the most abundant of the alkaline-earth metals and is the fifth most abundant element in Earth's crust. It is important in the formation of teeth and bones. Compounds of calcium are used in the manufacture of iron and steel.

Strontium-90 is a type of strontium that is radioactive—it breaks down and in the process emits radiation. Strontium-90 is a by-product of reactions that occur

This Bronze Age axe head was discovered in Sweden and dates from 2000–500 BCE. Bronze is a strong alloy and was useful for making tools and weapons.

THE METALS OF ANTIQUITY

Until the end of the 13th century, only seven metals were known—gold, copper, lead, silver, mercury, iron, and tin. These are called the metals of antiquity. Gold was the first of these metals to be discovered and has been in use since around 6000 BCE. For much of its history, gold has been used for decorative purposes, such as jewelry and ornaments, though it also is now used in electronic devices because it is a good conductor of electricity. Copper was in use by around 4200 BCE and was used for tools and weapons. Silver was first used around 4000 BCE and, like gold, was employed for decorative purposes. Around 3500 BCE, Romans were using lead for plumbing, and, around the same time in the Middle East, tin was being added to copper to make the alloy bronze. Alloys are materials made from two or more metals or a metal and a nonmetal. In the case of copper and tin, the resulting alloy is stronger than copper or tin alone. Iron smelting became a common process around 1200 BCE, though iron was known about long before this. In the ancient world, iron had many uses, such as weapons and farming implements. Mercury, also known as quicksilver, has been found in an Egyptian tomb of around 1500 BCE. It was used to form alloys with gold and silver.

COPPER CLEANER

Put some copper coins in a bowl containing some vinegar mixed with a teaspoon of table salt. After a few minutes, remove the coins from the salt and vinegar solution. What can you see? Copper coins gradually get dull over time. The copper in the coins reacts with oxygen in the air to form a layer of copper oxide over the surface of the coin. Pure copper is a bright, shiny metal, but copper oxide is dull and green. Vinegar contains a substance called acetic acid. The acid dissolves the copper oxide layer to reveal the shiny copper underneath.

in nuclear power stations and can be a very dangerous pollutant. It has a similar chemistry to calcium and so can take the place of calcium in bones. The radiation can cause damage to blood cells and may even cause death.

The silvery metal on this truck is a plating of chromium. Chromium is a transition metal that is used as a plating to give a hard, shiny, and rust-resistant finish.

GROUPS 3–12: TRANSITION METALS

The transition metals make up groups 3 through 12 of the periodic table. They include copper, iron, nickel, and zinc. Typically, transition metals are hard, with high melting points.

The chemistry of the transition metals is complex. Many lose one or more electrons from their outer electron shell when they react with other elements. Copper, for example, may lose one electron to form an ion with a single positive charge, or it may lose two electrons to form an ion with a positive charge of two.

Some transition metals have characteristic colors when they form compounds, such as the bright blue crystals of copper sulfate. Many are good electrical conductors because the electrons in the outer electron shell are not bound tightly to each atom. These electrons are therefore free to conduct electricity. Silver is the best conductor of all the metals.

Many transition metals have important uses. Iron is the most widely used and perhaps the most important

KEY TERMS

- **Alkali metals:** Those metals that form Group 1 of the periodic table.
- **Alkaline-earth metals:** Those metals that form Group 2 of the periodic table.
- **Alloys:** Alloys are made of a metal combined with one or more other metals or nonmetals such as carbon.
- **Radioactive element:** An element that breaks down and emits radiation in the process.
- **Transition metals:** Those metals that make up Groups 3 through 12 of the periodic table.

transition metal. Iron has been used for thousands of years to make tools and weapons. Today, almost all iron is made into an alloy called steel, which contains a mixture of iron with the nonmetal carbon. Steel is used to make buildings, automobiles, ships, bridges, and many other things.

Copper is also very important. Since it is such a good conductor, copper is used to make electrical cables and wires. It is also used to make pipes for water supplies in homes. Some copper is mixed with zinc to make an alloy called brass. Brass is a hard, yellow, shiny alloy commonly used to make decorative items.

UNUSUAL MERCURY

Mercury has been known for thousands of years. Early chemists, called alchemists, valued the dense liquid for its unusual properties. Early physicians used mercury as an antiseptic. An antiseptic is a substance that kills or restricts the growth of harmful germs. Since mercury expands evenly when heated, mercury is used in barometers and thermometers, though

the use of mercury in thermometers is becoming increasingly rare owing to health concerns. Although the metal is highly poisonous, mercury compounds are still valued for their antiseptic properties. Alloys made with mercury are called amalgams. Amalgams containing various compositions of mercury, zinc, tin, and copper are used in filling teeth.

The Mad Hatter is a character in Lewis Carroll's *Alice's Adventures in Wonderland* (1865). In real life, hat makers often suffered from mental disorders owing to the poisonous effects of the mercury they used for making felt for hats; hence the phrase "mad as a hatter."

Modern aircraft are made of many alloys. One of the most common metals used to make aircraft alloys is aluminum, which is light but strong.

GROUPS 13–16: OTHER METALS

Aluminum in Group 13 is the most abundant metal in Earth's crust. Like other Group 13 metals, aluminum may donate up to three electrons to other elements when forming compounds. Aluminum is made into food containers, drink cans, kitchen foil, saucepans, and many other objects. It is also a constituent of many alloys.

Group 14 contains two important metals—tin and lead. Both metals are used to make alloys. Bronze is an alloy of copper and tin. People made bronze tools and weapons thousands of years ago. Lead is an important ingredient of the alloys pewter and solder. Pewter is mainly a decorative alloy. Solder is commonly made of tin and lead. Increasingly, however, lead is being replaced in solder with other metals owing to safety issues concerning the use of lead. Lead was once used to make water pipes but lead is poisonous and many people suffered from lead poisoning as a consequence of this use. Lead is commonly used to make batteries and is a constituent of

ALLOYS

Steel consists of small amounts of carbon added to iron. Alloys are made of a metal combined with one or more other metals or nonmetals. These combinations can produce materials that have different qualities to their constituent materials. Brass is an alloy of copper and zinc that is more malleable than either of these two elements. It also has good acoustic properties that make it ideal for musical instruments such as trumpets and tubas. Iron on its own is strong but brittle. Adding carbon makes it flexible. Some materials need to have properties that metals alone do not provide. For example, aircraft need to be made of alloys that withstand stresses at high temperatures. Such alloys may contain more than ten different elements to achieve the desired results.

many types of glass, such as that used to make a type of fine glassware called lead crystal.

Bismuth is the only metal in Group 15. This pinkish metal is a poor conductor of electricity. Many chemists question whether bismuth is a metal or a metalloid. Polonium is a radioactive metal in Group 16. It is only found in tiny amounts in nature.

ALUMINUM

Aluminum was discovered in 1807 by the English scientist Humphry Davy (1778–1829). He was not, however, able to isolate a sample. This did not occur until 1825 when the Danish scientist Hans Christian Oersted (1777–1851) managed to produce minute quantities of this element. By the 1850s, techniques for producing more aluminum had been devised, but they were still very inefficient. Consequently, aluminum at this time was more expensive than gold. So precious was aluminum, that Napoleon III, Emperor of France, even used aluminum cutlery at state banquets. In 1886, a method was finally discovered for producing large quantities of aluminum: the Hall-Héroult process. If a powerful electric current is passed through a bath of a molten mineral called cryolite into which aluminum oxide has been dissolved, then molten aluminum settles at the bottom of the bath. This process was discovered independently by French metallurgist Paul Louis Toussaint Héroult (1863–1914) and U.S. chemist Charles Martin Hall (1863–1914). This method enabled the cheap production of aluminum and is the method by which most aluminum is produced today.

The metal object above left is called a die. Aluminum is heated until it becomes soft and is then forced through the gaps in the die. This process forms the long upright parts of a ladder, such as that on the right.

CHAPTER SIX

GASES AND NONMETALS

The nonmetal elements are Group 17 (the halogens), Group 18 (noble gases), and the following elements, in ascending atomic number: hydrogen, carbon, nitrogen, oxygen, phosphorus, sulfur, and selenium.

There are far fewer nonmetal elements than metal elements in the periodic table. However, the nonmetals far outweigh the metals in terms of abundance on Earth. Earth's atmosphere consists entirely of nonmetals, mostly nitrogen and oxygen, with tiny amounts of other gases. Oxygen, in combination with other elements, also makes up nearly half of Earth's crust. The nonmetals, particularly carbon, are vital for all living organisms to enable them to live, breathe, and grow. Without the nonmetals humans could not exist.

Nonmetals are everywhere. They make up the rocks on the seabed, the water of the oceans, the oxygen in the diver's tank, the bubbles of carbon dioxide rising to the surface, and most of the diver's body.

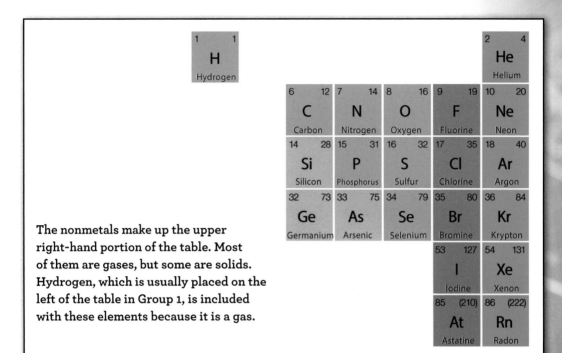

The nonmetals make up the upper right-hand portion of the table. Most of them are gases, but some are solids. Hydrogen, which is usually placed on the left of the table in Group 1, is included with these elements because it is a gas.

PHYSICAL CHARACTERISTICS

The nonmetals show a range of physical properties. At normal temperatures and pressures, most nonmetals are gases, a few are solids, and bromine is a liquid. Unlike metals, most nonmetals do not conduct heat and electricity very well. Their melting points are generally lower than those of metals. Solid nonmetals are also brittle and lack the characteristic shiny surfaces of metals.

REACTIVITY OF NONMETALS

Almost all nonmetals consist of small atoms with many electrons in their outer electron shell. The outer electron shell of the noble gases is full. As a result, the atoms of the noble gases are stable. They do not readily give up or share their electrons with the atoms of other elements. The outer electron shell of other nonmetal atoms is at least half full or nearly full. In most cases, nonmetals form compounds by accepting electrons or sharing electrons with other atoms. Adding or sharing electrons results in a full outer shell, which is more stable than a partially full outer shell. Nonmetals often accept electrons from metal atoms to form strongly bonded ionic compounds. With other nonmetals, they form bonds by sharing electrons (covalent bonds).

HYDROGEN: THE MOST COMMON ELEMENT

Hydrogen is the most common element in the universe. It is unique among the nonmetals. The atoms of this invisible, odorless

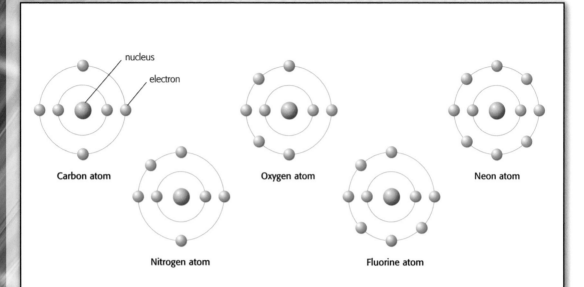

nucleus

electron

Carbon atom

Oxygen atom

Neon atom

Nitrogen atom

Fluorine atom

The outer electron shell of nonmetals ranges from half full (carbon) to completely full (neon). Nonmetals form a wide range of compounds by sharing electrons with other nonmetals or gaining electrons from other elements. Only neon, which has a full outer shell, does not react chemically.

gas are relatively small. Each one has just one electron in its outer electron shell. The hydrogen atom tends to donate this electron to the atoms of other elements during chemical reactions. In this way, it reacts more like a metal than a nonmetal. For this reason, hydrogen is usually placed above the Group 1 metals

Hydrogen is the lightest element, capable of supporting airships, but it is also highly flammable. In 1937, the German airship *Hindenburg* exploded, killing 36 people. Helium proved much safer.

on the left of the periodic table. Like many gaseous nonmetals, hydrogen is found as diatomic molecules (two atoms linked by a single bond) in nature. Natural gas is the main source of hydrogen on Earth.

Hydrogen is very explosive. The gas was once used to lift giant airships in the early 20th century. However, so many disasters occurred that all the hydrogen-inflated airships were taken out of service. Today, hydrogen is used to make a range of important chemicals, such as ammonia and acids, and has applications in the manufacture of margarine and as a fuel.

The most expensive allotropes in the world are the sparkling cut-diamond form of carbon.

SOLID, BUT NOT A METAL

Three nonmetals are solids at normal conditions. They are carbon (Group 14), phosphorus (Group 15), and sulfur (Group 16). All three elements exist in different structural forms, called allotropes. A substance is said to be an allotrope when two or more different forms occur in the same state, whether solid, liquid, or gas.

Carbon has several solid allotropes, including graphite and diamond. Each allotrope consists of a regular arrangement of carbon atoms. In diamond, this crystal structure is extremely stable. As a result, diamond is one of the hardest

ORGANIC CHEMISTRY

Carbon atoms can form bonds with many other carbon atoms. When other elements join with the carbon atoms, an almost endless variety of compounds can form. For example, hydrocarbons are compounds of carbon and hydrogen. Hydrocarbons form the basis of billion-dollar chemical industries, from paint to petroleum. More complex carbon compounds, such as carbohydrates and proteins, are the foundations for every living organism. Indeed, carbon makes up about 20 percent of the weight of the human body. The study of these carbon compounds is called organic chemistry. It is one of the largest and most important branches of chemistry.

KEY TERMS

- **Allotrope:** A different form of the same element in which the atoms are arranged in a different structure.
- **Lubricant:** A substance that helps surfaces slide past each other.
- **Ozone:** A form of oxygen in which three oxygen atoms join to form a molecule.
- **Photosynthesis:** A chemical reaction in which plants use energy from the sun to change carbon dioxide and water into food.

Matches contain two nonmetal elements—sulfur and phosphorus. The sulfur is in the match head. The phosphorus is coated along the side of the box. Striking the match energizes the phosphorus and ignites the sulfur and other chemicals in the head.

substances known in nature. Diamonds are therefore useful in cutting tools. They are also highly prized as gemstones.

By contrast, the crystals of graphite form layers that move over one another easily. Graphite is sometimes used as a lubricant, thanks to the sliding properties of its crystals. Graphite is also mixed with clay and used as the "lead" in pencils. It is also the only nonmetallic element that conducts electricity.

The two most important phosphorus allotropes are the white and red forms. An allotrope called black phosphorus exists, but it can only be made under high pressure. Similar to carbon, phosphorus allotropes differ in their crystal structure. White phosphorus is

Plants such as these (uprooted) peanuts need phosphorus and nitrogen to grow. Peanuts have nodules on their roots where bacteria live that can convert nitrogen into a usable form.

STINKY SULFUR

While pure sulfur is odorless, this element has a tendency to form some extremely smelly compounds. The gas hydrogen sulfide (H_2S) is perhaps the most familiar, with its smell of rotten eggs. This smell is often encountered in wells or water systems contaminated with bacteria that produce hydrogen sulfide. It is also released from oil wells, volcanoes, and some thermal springs. Hydrogen sulfide is perhaps better known to many schoolchildren as the main ingredient in stink bombs.

Sulfur also occurs in many organic compounds, especially substances called thiols, or mercaptans. Thiols are responsible for the smells of garlic, boiled cabbage, bad breath, and rotting flesh. Thiols are also used to great effect by animals such as skunks, which spray thiols to warn off predators. However, thiols can be useful—gas companies add a tiny amount to odorless natural gas so that people can detect a gas leak. Not all thiols smell bad. Some of the aromas in wine and the smell of grapefruits are also produced by thiols.

the most reactive allotrope. This waxy solid is stored under oil or water to prevent it from reacting with oxygen in the air. White phosphorus is used to create smoke screens during military operations. Red phosphorus is much more stable than white phosphorus.

It is used to make safety matches and fireworks. Like carbon, phosphorus is an important element in living organisms, particularly as the phosphates in bones and teeth, and also in the process of photosynthesis in plants. Photosynthesis is the process by which plants convert carbon dioxide and water into food.

Sulfur is the ninth most abundant element on Earth. It is often found combined with useful metals in the form of ores. Underground deposits of pure sulfur are also common around hot springs and volcanoes.

Elemental sulfur (sulfur in its pure, uncombined state) usually occurs as pale yellow crystals. However, chemists have identified up to eight different allotropes. Sulfur is an extremely important

Skunks are given a wide berth by anyone who comes into contact with them, especially when a skunk raises its tail to spray. The foul smell of the sulfur-containing spray is so powerful, only a few drops are necessary to deter predators or people.

DIATOMIC MOLECULES

Diatomic molecules are compounds in which two nonmetal atoms, whether the same or different elements, are joined by the attraction of sharing electrons (covalent bonds). In nature, seven nonmetals occur as diatomic elements. These nonmetals are hydrogen (H_2), nitrogen (N_2), oxygen (O_2), fluorine (F_2), chlorine (Cl_2), bromine (Br_2), and iodine (I_2). Earth's atmosphere consists almost entirely (99 percent) of diatomic oxygen and nitrogen. Other examples of diatomic molecules include carbon monoxide (CO), hydrogen fluoride (HF), and nitric oxide (NO).

element in the chemical industry. Most is used to make sulfuric acid. Other uses include the manufacture of detergents, rubber, explosives, petroleum, and many other essential products.

EARTH'S MAIN GASES

Nitrogen and oxygen are the two main gases in Earth's atmosphere. About 78 percent of the volume of the atmosphere is nitrogen and 21 percent is oxygen. Most of the nitrogen and oxygen used in the chemical industry is taken from the air. At room temperature, nitrogen is a colorless, odorless, unreactive gas because of its tendency to form diatomic molecules. It has many applications, ranging from the manufacture of ammonia and nitric acid to its use in dyes, explosives, and fertilizers. Liquid nitrogen is used as a refrigerant by many industries and to keep medical samples frozen.

Like many nonmetals, nitrogen is an important part of the chemistry of living organisms. Many molecules in the human body contain nitrogen atoms. Humans obtain nitrogen by eating plants, which in turn extract it from the soil.

One way that nitrogen enters the soil is during thunderstorms, when lightning forces nitrogen and oxygen atoms in the air to react and form nitrogen oxides, which are then washed into the soil by rain. Soil bacteria can also convert atmospheric nitrogen into compounds called nitrates. The nitrates are then taken up by plants.

In nature, both nitrogen and oxygen are usually found as diatomic molecules (see box above). Oxygen also exists as the molecule ozone (O_3), which is a combination of three oxygen atoms. Like nitrogen, oxygen is an invisible, odorless gas. Many substances react with oxygen in the air when they are left out in the open. Burning simply involves heating a substance in the air. The substance then reacts with the oxygen in the air.

Oxygen is stored as a liquid and mainly used in the steelmaking industry. Liquid oxygen is also used as a rocket fuel. Naturally, oxygen is vital to animals since they need it to breathe. Plants produce oxygen during a process called photosynthesis.

THE HIGHLY REACTIVE HALOGENS

The halogens form Group 17 of the periodic table. At room temperature, the physical

Carl Scheele was the first to find that heating oxides gave off a gas.

Antoine Lavoisier made the key connection between oxygen and burning.

Joseph Priestley's work provided the basis for Lavoisier's experiments.

WHO DISCOVERED OXYGEN?

In the early 1770s, scientists were trying to understand the chemistry of combustion (burning). Many thought that matter contained a substance called phlogiston. As substances burned, phlogiston was thought to pour into the air. The phlogiston theory was also used to explain how animals breathed and metals rusted. In 1772, Swedish chemist Carl Wilhelm Scheele (1742–1786) experimented with combustion by heating metal oxides and noted that an invisible gas was given off. Two years later, English chemist Joseph Priestley (1733–1804) also made the same discovery. Neither Priestley nor Scheele realized how close they were to the truth. This was left to French chemist Antoine-Laurent Lavoisier (1743–1794). Lavoisier was also doing experiments in combustion in Paris, France. He was convinced that the phlogiston theory was wrong. When he heard about Priestley's experiments, Lavoisier realized that the invisible gas was responsible for combustion. Lavoisier noted that the gas formed acidic compounds with many substances. He named it oxygine, from the Greek words meaning "acid former." Lavoisier took all the credit for himself. The role of Scheele and Priestley was ignored for many years.

SELENIUM

Selenium is the third nonmetal in Group 16 of the periodic table. In nature, selenium is almost always found mixed with sulfur and metals such as copper and lead. As a pure element, selenium exists in one of many different forms, called allotropes. In some cases, selenium occurs as a red powder or black, glassy solid. Selenium can also exist as red crystals. The most common allotrope looks like a gray, metallic solid. Due to its metal-like appearance, some chemists think that the element is a metalloid. Metalloids have properties similar to both metals and nonmetals in different circumstances.

properties of the halogens vary from solid iodine, through liquid bromine, to the gases fluorine and chlorine. The chemical properties are typical of nonmetals. The halogens usually take in an electron from the atoms of other elements. They are highly reactive, and fluorine is the most reactive element of all. For example, the halogens readily react with the alkali metals to form ionic compounds. The atom of the alkali metal donates one electron to the atom of the halogen, resulting in a stable ionic compound. Common salt (sodium chloride) is perhaps the most familiar example. Its chemical formula is NaCl.

The halogens have many different uses. Chlorine is sometimes added to swimming pools to kill harmful germs in the water. Fluorine is often found in toothpastes and drinking water because it is thought to help strengthen the teeth and bones. Iodine is a dark-purple solid, and is an essential nutrient in the human diet. It is also often used as a mild antiseptic, helping to kill or restrict the growth of harmful germs on the skin.

Swimming pools often use chlorine or chlorine dioxide as a disinfectant to kill any germs that may be lurking in the water.

THE NONREACTIVE NOBLE GASES

The noble gases form Group 18 (sometimes called Group

0) of the periodic table. All of this group are gases at normal room temperature, and they all have low boiling points. The outer electron shell of each noble gas is full. The atoms are stable and do not normally react with the atoms of other elements.

The noble gases used to be called the "inert" gases. The word *inert* means "totally unreactive." This implies that the gases do not react with any other substances. In laboratory conditions, however, xenon has been made to react with fluorine. The word *noble* is now the accepted term for gases in Group 18. In chemistry and alchemy, the word *noble* has also been used to describe metals that do not react with oxygen.

The noble gases have a number of important uses. Helium is an invisible, odorless gas. Since it is unreactive and much lighter than air and safer than hydrogen, it is an ideal gas for inflating hot-air balloons and airships. Scientists are also interested in liquid helium because it has some strange and unusual properties. It does not boil and cannot be made solid by reducing the temperature. At very low temperatures, it can even defy gravity and creep up and over the walls of its container.

Neon lighting is another valuable application of the noble gases. Neon is usually used to make brightly colored lights, but xenon and krypton lights are also popular. Xenon also fills the flash-tubes of stroboscopic (flashing on and off) equipment. Photography flashlights are increasingly filled with krypton. Argon is often used to prevent metals from oxidizing during welding.

Lightbulbs are filled with gases that glow when they are switched on. Many of these gases are noble gases, such as neon, krypton, or xenon. Halogens are also used in many types of lights, such as in car headlights and fog lamps, where they give off a brilliant white light.

CHAPTER SEVEN

THE METALLOIDS: BETWEEN METALS AND NONMETALS

Some elements look like metals, but they are brittle and do not conduct heat or electricity very well. These elements, called metalloids, lie between the metals and nonmetals in the periodic table.

An imaginary line drawn diagonally across groups 13, 14, and 15 of the periodic table separates the metals from the nonmetals. Elements on the left of the line are metals. Elements on the right are nonmetals. The elements that make up the line itself are boron (5), silicon (14), germanium (32), arsenic (33), antimony (51), and tellurium (52). These elements are called metalloids, or semimetals. This classification is not very precise—some chemists include bismuth (83), polonium (84), and astatine (85) in the metalloid group.

PHYSICAL CHARACTERISTICS

Metalloids have some of the properties of metals and some of nonmetals. As a result, they show

The large rectangular gray component on this circuit board is made of the metalloid silicon and is called a silicon chip. Silicon and other metalloids, such as germanium and arsenic, are important materials in the electronics industries.

a wide range of properties. For example, the surface of a piece of arsenic is shiny like a metal. Unlike most metals, however, arsenic is a rather weak solid—arsenic is brittle and a chunk of arsenic breaks easily. True metals rarely form compounds with other metals. Arsenic readily forms compounds with metals. Arsenopyrite, for example, is a compound made of iron, arsenic, and sulfur and has the chemical formula FeAsS. Arsenopyrite is the most common naturally occurring mineral that contains arsenic.

Some metalloids act both as electrical conductors and insulators. In some circumstances, they will conduct

5	11	6	12	7	14	8	16
B		**C**		**N**		**O**	
Boron		Carbon		Nitrogen		Oxygen	
13	27	14	28	15	31	16	32
Al		**Si**		**P**		**S**	
Aluminum		Silicon		Phosphorus		Sulfur	
31	70	32	73	33	75	34	79
Ga		**Ge**		**As**		**Se**	
Gallium		Germanium		Arsenic		Selenium	
49	115	50	119	51	122	52	128
In		**Sn**		**Sb**		**Te**	
Indium		Tin		Antimony		Tellurium	
81	204	82	207	83	209	84	(209)
Tl		**Pb**		**Bi**		**Po**	
Thallium		Lead		Bismuth		Polonium	

The metalloids (orange) form a diagonal across the periodic table and divide the metals (yellow) from the nonmetals (blue).

electricity and in others they will not. Substances that behave in this way are called semiconductors. Boron, germanium, and silicon are the most important semiconductors.

BLACK, BRITTLE BORON

Boron is the first element in Group 13 of the periodic table. Credit for its discovery usually goes to French chemists Joseph-Louis Gay-Lussac (1778–1850) and Louis-Jacques Thénard (1777–1857) in 1808. English chemist Humphry Davy (1778–1829) also made the discovery independently in the same year. Boron is a black, brittle, shiny solid. It is extremely hard, and for this reason it may be added to steel and other alloys to make them even harder. Boron and its compounds have many other uses. Boric acid, or borax, is an important compound of boron. Borax is a mild antiseptic that stops harmful germs from growing on the skin. Borax is also widely used in industry, for example, in leather tanning and glassmaking. Boron is also an essential trace element for plants.

JUST WHAT MENDELEEV EXPECTED: GERMANIUM

The discovery of germanium (Group 14) is an important event in the history of the periodic table. When Mendeleev drew up his 1869 table in order of atomic mass, he left some gaps in it. He suggested that the gaps would be filled by new elements that were unknown to scientists of the

The white islands on this lake in Bolivia are deposits of borax. Borax is a major source of the metalloid boron.

time. He also predicted the exact chemical properties of the new elements.

In 1886, German chemist Clemens Winkler (1838–1904) discovered a new element, which he called germanium. The discovery matched Mendeleev's prediction for one such element, which he had called eka-silicon because it would sit underneath silicon in the periodic table.

Like all the metalloids, germanium is a brittle solid with a shiny surface. Like boron and silicon, it is used as a semiconductor in the electronics industry. It is also used to make glass lenses for cameras and microscopes.

CRUST, CLAY, QUARTZ, SAND, AND GLASS: SILICON

Silicon is found underneath carbon in Group 14 of the periodic table. Around 30 percent of Earth's crust consists of silicon. Pure silicon is a hard, gray solid with a shiny surface. In nature, however, silicon is found combined with oxygen in the form of silicon dioxide (SiO_2), also known as silica. Silica is the most abundant compound in Earth's crust. Silica can take many forms but the most common is quartz. Clay commonly contains silica, and in many places silica is the

SEMICONDUCTORS

The outer electrons in a metal's atoms are not tightly bound to the nucleus. They can move freely through the metal. This movement of electrons makes up an electrical current, and therefore metals are good conductors. By contrast, the atoms of nonmetals hold on very tightly to their electrons. The electrons cannot move about as freely, and nonmetals are insulators.

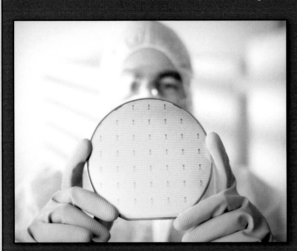

Pure silicon is an insulator at low temperatures. The electrons in the silicon atoms are used to form bonds with neighboring silicon atoms. As the temperature rises, however, the electrons break free from the bonds. These electrons can then move through the silicon, and electricity can flow. For this reason, silicon is called a semiconductor.

Silicon can also be made a better conductor by adding small amounts of other substances, such as phosphorus and boron. This process is called doping. Although silicon conducts electricity under the right conditions, it will never conduct electricity as well as a metal.

This circular wafer of silicon is used to make silicon chips. Silicon chips contain thousands of tiny electrical components that take advantage of silicon's properties as a semiconductor.

main component of sand. Sand is made mostly of tiny pieces of quartz and is an important building material. Quartz is heated and shaped to make glass.

Silicones are another valuable group of silicon products. Lubricants, varnishes, adhesives, cosmetics, and many other goods are made using silicones.

SILICON CHIPS POWER THE DIGITAL REVOLUTION

By far the most important use for silicon is in the semiconductor industry.

Citrine is a form of yellow quartz (silicon dioxide). Quartz can take several different forms, such as amethyst (purple) and rose quartz (pink).

METALLOID MURDER

The poisonous effects of arsenic have been known since at least Roman times. Arsenic was often used as a means of murdering people, whether to settle scores or for political reasons. Its great advantages as an instrument of murder are that it is colorless, odorless, and tasteless. Also, the effects of arsenic poisoning are similar to food poisoning. The victim experiences severe abdominal cramps, vomiting, diarrhea and, if the dose is large enough, death from shock. Throughout history, there have been many famous poisoners who used arsenic. In Italy, during the Middle Ages, members of the Borgia family were notorious for poisoning their political opponents. In 19th-century England, the serial killer Mary Anne Cotton used arsenic in cups of tea to murder at least 21 people, including three of her husbands and several of her children. In the 1830s, English chemist James Marsh devised a test for arsenic that enabled scientists to detect whether someone had been poisoned using this metalloid. Following this invention, arsenic poisoning as a means of murder fell out of favor.

Arsenic is poisonous and is no longer as freely available as it once was. Today, it is used in the electronics industry to make semiconductors. A compound of arsenic, arsenic trioxide, is used to treat leukemia.

FISHER LABORATORY CHEMICAL
Cat.No. A-892   1 lb.(453 g.)

Arsenic Metal 75?
Crystal — Purified

As   F. W. 74.91

❊ POISON ❊
FISHER SCIENTIFIC COMPANY
MANUFACTURING CHEMISTS — FAIR LAWN, N. J.
FOR LABORATORY USE ONLY   MADE IN U.S.A.

Silicon is used to make a wide range of electronic parts. Wafer-thin slices of silicon, called silicon chips, are an integral part of computers. The chips contain tiny electrical circuits that control the microprocessor—the computer's brain.

The first computers were enormous machines that filled entire rooms.

KEY TERMS

- **Antiseptic:** A substance that kills or restricts the growth of harmful germs.
- **Conductor:** A substance through which heat or electricity flow easily.
- **Insulator:** A substance that is a poor conductor of heat or electricity.
- **Microprocessor:** A tiny silicon chip that contains all the electronic circuits used to run a computer. The microprocessor is the computer's "brain."
- **Semiconductor:** A substance that conducts heat and electricity but only in certain circumstances.

TELLURIUM

Tellurium has a special place in the history of the periodic table. Around 1860, French geologist Alexandre-Emile Bèguyer de Chancourtois (1820–1886) arranged the known elements in a spiral around a cylinder. He placed the elements in order of atomic weight. De Chancourtois called his arrangement the "telluric spiral" because tellurium was situated in the center of the spiral. Tellurium is a rare silvery white metalloid with a shiny metal-like surface, but it is also extremely brittle. Tellurium is added to alloys to improve the strength and wear of the alloy.

A compound of tellurium is used in the solar cells that cover the roof of this gas station. Enough energy is obtained from these solar cells to power the gas pumps and light the station.

Impressive as they were at the time, these early computers could perform the same tasks as a handheld calculator can today. Silicon chips have revolutionized electronics. The chips themselves are cut from a single silicon crystal. Millions of tiny components, called transistors, are then etched on the silicon using lasers. The resulting silicon chip can then be used to control an electronic device. The chip is often called an integrated circuit because it integrates (connects) all the electronics on a single piece of silicon.

HIGHLY TOXIC ANTIMONY

Antimony is most commonly found in the mineral stibnite. Antimony has been known of in compounds since ancient times, when it was used in cosmetics and medicines. It has been regarded as a metalloid element since at least the 17th century. Antimony and many of its compounds are highly toxic. It has many industrial uses, such as in semiconductors, in alloys that expand when they solidify, and in the manufacture of enamels. It is also used in lead alloys that are used to make lead batteries.

CHAPTER EIGHT

RARE-EARTH METALS: THE LANTHANIDES AND ACTINIDES

The rare-earth metals form two rows of elements below the main body of the periodic table. The first row contains the lanthanides (lanthanum to lutetium). The second row contains the actinides (actinium to lawrencium).

The black sand of this beach is made of monazite, a mineral that contains a high proportion of rare-earth elements.

Look at the periodic table. Follow the elements along Period 6. The period starts with cesium (55), then barium (56). The atomic number then jumps to hafnium (72) and continues in sequence until radon (86) at the end of the row. The same thing happens in Period 7. After francium (87) and radium (88), the atomic number jumps to rutherfordium (104). It then continues until element 118 at the end of the row.

The missing elements lanthanum (57) to lutetium (71) and actinium (89) to lawrencium (103) appear in two separate rows at the bottom of the periodic table. The elements in the first row are called the lanthanide elements. The elements in the second row are called the actinide elements. Together these elements are called the rare-earth metals.

PHYSICAL CHARACTERISTICS

The rare earths share many common properties. For this reason, it is often difficult to tell them apart. All are silvery

57	139	58	140	59	141	60	144	61	(145)	62	150	63	152	64	157	65	159	66	163	67	165	68	167	69	169	70	173	71	175
La		Ce		Pr		Nd		Pm		Sm		Eu		Gd		Tb		Dy		Ho		Er		Tm		Yb		Lu	
Lanthanum		Cerium		Praseodymium		Neodymium		Promethium		Samarium		Europium		Gadolinium		Terbium		Dysprosium		Holmium		Erbium		Thulium		Ytterbium		Lutetium	
89	(227)	90	232	91	231	92	238	93	(237)	94	(244)	95	243	96	(247)	97	(247)	98	(251)	99	(252)	100	(257)	101	(258)	102	(259)	103	(262)
Ac		Th		Pa		U		Np		Pu		Am		Cm		Bk		Cf		Es		Fm		Md		No		Lr	
Actinium		Thorium		Protactinium		Uranium		Neptunium		Plutonium		Americium		Curium		Berkelium		Californium		Einsteinium		Fermium		Mendelevium		Nobelium		Lawrencium	

white to gray solids with shiny surfaces, but they tarnish (discolor) in the air. The discoloration occurs because the metals readily react with oxygen in the air. The oxygen combines with the metal to form a compound called a metal oxide. The thin layer of metal oxide coats the surface of the metal. Like most metals, the rare earths are good conductors of heat and electricity.

In nature, many rare-earth metals occur mixed with other elements to form rocks and minerals. Minerals that contain valuable elements are called ores. Because the rare earths are all so similar in their chemical properties, they often occur together and are difficult to separate. Monazite is an ore of several mixed rare-earth metals and the elements phosphorus and oxygen. The rare-earth metals are often found in combination with nonmetals. Each metal atom gives up three electrons in its outer electron shell to form chemical bonds with the nonmetal atom. In some cases, the atom may lose just two or four outer electrons, forming compounds with different properties.

This 1930s poster is advertising a face cream that contains thorium, a radioactive rare-earth element. The cream also contains another radioactive element, radium. Both were once thought to be beneficial to health!

The rare-earth metals usually sit as a separate block at the bottom of the periodic table.

THE LANTHANIDES

The name rare-earth metal is slightly misleading for the lanthanide elements. The lanthanides are not as rare as chemists first thought. Some lanthanides are more common than better-known metals such as platinum or lead, for example. Only promethium has to be made artificially.

The lanthanides are relatively soft metals, but their hardness increases as

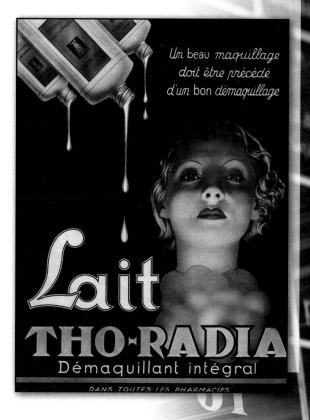

Un beau *maquillage* doit être précédé d'un bon *démaquillage*

Lait

THO-RADIA

Démaquillant intégral

DANS TOUTES LES PHARMACIES

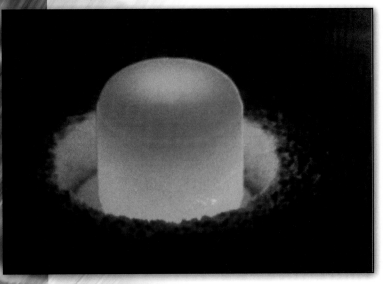

This pellet of plutonium glows with radioactivity. Plutonium forms as part of the decay process of uranium. Plutonium is used as a fuel source for space probes and in nuclear power plants. It is highly toxic and dangerous even at very low quantities.

KEY TERMS

- Alloy: Mixture of two or more metals or a metal and a nonmetal such as carbon.
- Boiling point: The temperature at which a liquid turns into a gas.
- Melting point: The temperature at which a solid turns into a liquid.
- Ore: Mineral that contains useful elements such as aluminum or copper.
- Radioactivity: The release of energy that results when the nucleus of an atom breaks down.
- Transuranium elements: Elements with an atomic number greater than that of uranium, which is 92.

the atomic number increases from left to right across the period. Lanthanides have a high melting and boiling point, and they are extremely reactive. The lanthanides react readily with most nonmetals. Generally, they lose three outer electrons to form bonds with nonmetal atoms. They react with water and weak acids and burn easily in air.

The lanthanides and their compounds have many uses. Some are useful catalysts, speeding up chemical reactions in the petroleum industry. Others are used to make lasers and fluorescent lamps. They are also used in televisions in the screen coatings that provide colored images. Some lanthanides are mixed with other metals to make alloys. The lanthanide metal adds to the strength of the final alloy. Some rare earths also have magnetic properties that are useful at extremely low temperatures where other magnetic elements do not work.

THE ACTINIDES

The actinide elements are dense, radioactive metals. Over time, their atoms break down to form the atoms of other elements. Some are very unstable and will only form compounds with elements that increase their stability. Like most metals, the actinides react with weak acids to release hydrogen. This gas is also given off when the actinides are placed in boiling water. The actinides react readily with oxygen in the air, which discolors the metal with a thin layer of metal oxide.

Uranium is the most common element of the actinides and is widely distributed around the world. It usually occurs as an oxide, uranium dioxide, UO_2. As the most abundant radioactive element, uranium is mined and processed for use in the nuclear power industry. Some uranium is also used to make a luminous yellowy green glass. Thorium also occurs in many parts of the world in the mineral monazite and may be even more common than uranium. Thorium is mainly used in the making of mantles for gas lamps, but also has uses as a catalyst in the production of nitric and sulfuric acids and in the oil industry. Thorium, too, has potential for use as a nuclear fuel. The other actinide elements have limited uses. Plutonium is used to power heart pacemakers and in the nuclear industry. Americium is used in smoke detectors.

SYNTHETIC ACTINIDES

Only the first four elements in the actinide series occur in any significant quantity in nature. These are actinium, thorium, protactinium, and uranium. Actinides with an atomic number greater than 92 (uranium) are known as the transuranium elements. Of these, only neptunium and plutonium have been found in nature, and even then only in trace amounts. All the other transuranium elements are synthetic elements made in the laboratory.

Edwin McMillan (1907–1991) was one of the scientists who discovered neptunium, which follows uranium in the actinide series. He shared the Nobel Prize for this discovery with Glenn Seaborg in 1951.

In 1940, American physicists Edwin McMillan (1907–1991) and Philip Abelson (1913–2004) produced an element with the atomic number 93. They named the element neptunium. A year later, U.S. chemist Glenn T. Seaborg (1912–1999) and his colleagues produced element 94, named plutonium. In

GLENN THEODORE SEABORG

Glenn Theodore Seaborg was born in Ishpeming, Michigan, on April 19, 1912. When he was a child, the family moved to Los Angeles, California. Seaborg studied at the University of California, Los Angeles (UCLA). He graduated in 1934 with a degree in chemistry. He then did postgraduate studies at the University of California, Berkeley. There, he studied with some of the leading scientists of the day, including American chemist Gilbert Lewis (1875–1946). Seaborg's research continued at Berkeley. Eventually, he became professor of chemistry.

It was during World War II (1939–1945) that Seaborg made his mark on the periodic table. In addition to plutonium, Seaborg discovered the elements americium, curium, berkelium, californium, einsteinium, fermium, mendelevium, and nobelium. In recognition of his contribution to chemistry, Seaborg shared the 1951 Nobel Prize with Edwin McMillan. Seaborg died in 1999, following complications after a stroke. The element seaborgium (106) is named in his honor.

Professor Glenn Seaborg was one of the most active researchers in the field of actinide elements.

1944, after more transuranium elements were discovered, Seaborg suggested that these elements should form a group similar to the lanthanide series. He called the new group the actinide series and placed both the lanthanides and actinides in a block at the bottom of the periodic table. Seaborg's revision was the last major change to the layout of the table.

THE HEAVIEST ELEMENTS

The search for even heavier elements than seaborgium has continued since the 1970s. Much of the work has been carried out at laboratories in Darmstadt in Germany, Dubna in Russia, and Berkeley in California. Because these elements do not occur naturally they have to be created.

The key to the process of making a new element lies in the ratio of protons and neutrons in the nucleus of an atom. If the ratio is not correct, the nucleus becomes unstable and the atom breaks apart. Certain combinations of protons and neutrons are very stable and are called "magic" numbers. The most stable heavy element

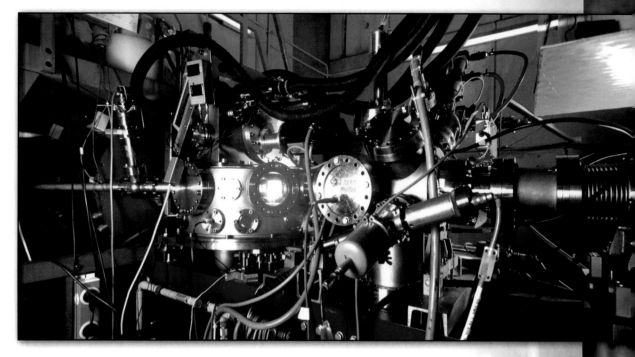

This equipment at Darmstadt in Germany is used to fuse heavy atoms together to form new elements.

in nature is lead, with 82 protons and 126 neutrons. Beyond this ideal ratio, researchers have predicted other combinations of protons and neutrons that could result in new "superheavy" elements. Researchers prepare them by bombarding one heavy element, such as americium or curium, with another rich in neutrons. That starts a fusion reaction that begins a radioactive decay chain. The presence of the new element is detected by analyzing the products that form. Using this method the elements bohrium (107), hassium (108), meitnerium (109), darmstadtium (110), roentgenium (111), copernicum (112), ununtrium (113), flevorium (114), ununpentium (115), livermorium (116), ununseptium (117), and ununoctium (118) have been discovered.

In theory chemists think that the maximum atomic number possible (the number of protons the nucleus can hold) lies somewhere between 170 and 210. However, it is doubtful whether chemists will actually identify such a large number of elements. The laws of science do not rule out the possibility of 210 protons in an atom, but the stability of the nucleus does. In fact, chemists may be close to finding all the elements of the periodic table. They think the maximum atomic number is about 120, which means there may be only two new elements left to be discovered.

CHAPTER NINE

BIOGRAPHY: DMITRI MENDELEEV

Dmitri Mendeleev overcame childhood deprivation and illness to become professor of chemistry at the University of St. Petersburg, Russia. As the formulator of the periodic table of elements, he is one of the founding figures of modern chemistry. He predicted the existence of several elements, unknown at the time, which have subsequently been discovered. Element no. 101 is named mendelevium for him.

Dmitri Mendeleev was the youngest of 14 children. When he was born, his father was principal of the gymnasium (high school) at Tobolsk in the Russian province of Siberia, but he became blind soon after Dmitri's birth. It was left to Mendeleev's mother to provide for the family. This she did by reopening an old glassworks that had belonged to her father. Mendeleev attended school, and showed particular talent in mathematics, physics, and geography.

Tragedy struck the family in 1847 with the death of Mendeleev's father. Soon after his death, the glass factory burned down, and the family moved 1,400 miles (2,250 km) to Moscow in an attempt to improve their fortunes. However, Mendeleev's recommendations from an obscure Siberian high school were unable to secure him entry to any Moscow educational institution, so the family moved again, this time

"In science we all must submit not to what seems to us attractive from one point of view or from another, but to what represents an agreement between theory and experiment...."

Dmitri Mendeleev
Faraday Lecture, the Royal Institution, London (1889)

to St. Petersburg, the Russian capital. Here, through the intervention of an old family friend, Mendeleev at last won a place at the Pedagogical Institute, a center for teacher training. But further tragedy followed soon after with the death of his mother and sister. Mendeleev himself contracted the lung disease tuberculosis (TB) and was given only six months to live. Despite this, he qualified as a teacher in 1855 and was posted to Odessa, a town on the Black Sea in southern Russia.

Two years later, he returned to study for a degree in chemistry at the University of St. Petersburg. In 1859, the Russian government sponsored him on a scholarship to Western Europe. He continued his chemistry studies at the University of Heidelberg, Germany, and made contact with leading chemists in Germany and France. He returned to Russia in 1861 and was made professor of chemistry at the St. Petersburg Technical Institute in 1864. Two years later he was appointed professor at the university. He devoted himself almost entirely to study of the elements.

Dimitri Mendeleev works in his office in St. Petersburg, Russia, in 1903.

Elements are substances that cannot be broken down into anything simpler by chemical means; all other substances are formed from them. French chemist Antoine Lavoisier (1743–1794) had been the first person to describe and define elements. Since then chemists had identified and given names to a catalog of elements that make up the physical world. At first, the elements were listed in order of their date of discovery. As more were found, they were grouped according to their chemical properties—that is, whether they were gases or solids, metals

KEY DATES	
1834	February 8, born in Tobolsk, Siberia, Russia
1849	Leaves Siberia with mother, travels first to Moscow and then to St. Petersburg
1855	Posted to teach in the Crimea
1856	Obtains advanced degree in chemistry in St. Petersburg
1859–61	Studies chemistry in France and Germany
1864	Becomes professor of chemistry at the St. Petersburg Technical Institute
1866	Appointed professor of chemistry at the University of St. Petersburg
1867	Makes study of French chemical industry that will help in later work in Russian soda and petroleum industries
1868–70	Publishes *The Principles of Chemistry*
1890	Retires from St. Petersburg University after a clash with the Russian government
1893	Appointed director of the Bureau of Weights and Measures
1907	February 2, dies in St. Petersburg

or nonmetals. But chemists in the 19th century still did not understand the relationship between the elements, or why they behave as they do.

JOHN DALTON: FOUNDER OF MODERN ATOMIC THEORY

A major contribution to understanding the elements was made by John Dalton (1790–1844), the founder of modern atomic theory. An interest in meteorology (weather patterns) led Dalton to study atmospheric gases such as hydrogen, nitrogen, and oxygen. Some gases, he found, dissolve more readily than others in water. These, he suggested, were the denser (heavier) gases. To explain how gases have different weights, Dalton developed the idea, first suggested by the Greek philosopher Democritus (*c.* 460–*c.* 370 BCE), that all matter consists of atoms. Dalton proposed that an atom is the smallest part of any element, and cannot be created or destroyed. The atoms of a particular element are identical to each other, and differ from those of other elements, especially in weight.

MAKING CONNECTIONS

Building on Dalton's work, other scientists began to look for connections between the atomic weights and chemical properties of substances. It was known, for example, that chlorine (Cl), bromine (Br), and iodine (I) are all very reactive (that is, they readily enter into chemical reactions). German chemist Johann Döbereiner (1780–1849) discovered that the atomic weight of one of them (bromine) is the average of the other two. He reckoned that chlorine had an atomic weight of 35 and iodine of 127, giving an average of 81; the actual

John Dalton's 1806-07 diagram of the atomic formulas for water and ammonia appears above. Dalton's table of elements was based on their weight (hydrogen is the lightest). Beside each element's name appeared its chemical symbol devised by Dalton. Below the table were some of his notations of simple compounds, and models repesenting different types of atoms, which Dalton visualized as solid particles.

atomic weight of bromine is just under 80. Döbereiner was able to find two other groups of three elements with a similar structure. Other chemists noted that elements with similar properties had similar weights. Again, they were using less precise values than modern scientists. They saw that iron (Fe, 56), cobalt (Co, 59), and nickel (Ni, 58) are hard, magnetic metals; ruthenium (Ru, 102), rhodium (Rh, 103), and palladium (Pd, 106) are very hard, easily shaped by hammering (ductile), and resistant to tarnish. It seemed possible that they might be able to start arranging the elements systematically.

MENDELEEV'S TABLE

When Mendeleev became professor at St. Petersburg University, he found there was no suitable textbook of general chemistry, so he began to write *The Principles of Chemistry* (1868–70). As he attempted to explain the relationships between the properties of elements, he decided to see if he could devise a system of classifying them. He started by writing them down in increasing order of their atomic weight, as accurately as he could measure it. He started with lithium (Li), a reactive metal. He saw that the seventh and

THE PERIODIC TABLE

The modern version of the periodic table shows all the elements that have been discovered or made, with their atomic weights. They are arranged in order of their atomic numbers in seven horizontal periods of varying length. Two very long periods of 14 elements each, 57–71 (the lanthanides) and 89–103 (the actinides), are displayed in separate lines below.

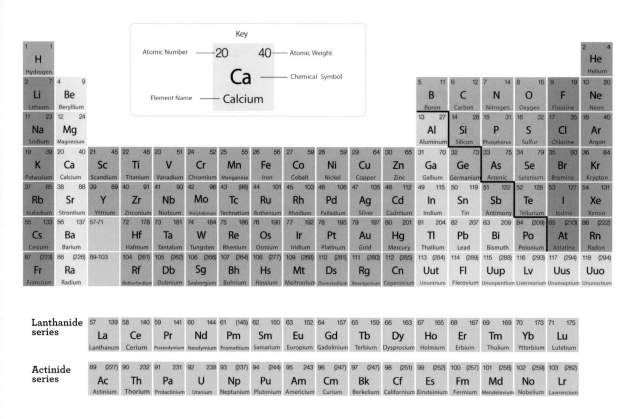

Mendeleev's first periodic table (opposite page) and a modern version (above). The notation system that uses a letter or letters as the symbol for each element (for example, Fe = iron; S = sulfur) was introduced by Swedish chemist J. J. Berzelius (1779–1848) in 1812.

— 70 —

но въ ней, мнѣ кажется, уже ясно выражается примѣнимость вы
ставляемаго мною начала ко всей совокупности элементовъ, пай
которыхъ извѣстенъ съ достовѣрностію. На этотъ разъ я и желалъ
преимущественно найдти общую систему элементовъ. Вотъ этотъ
опытъ:

$$
\begin{array}{lllllll}
 & & & Ti=50 & Zr=90 & ?=180. \\
 & & & V=51 & Nb=94 & Ta=182. \\
 & & & Cr=52 & Mo=96 & W=186. \\
 & & & Mn=55 & Rh=104{,}_4 & Pt=197{,}_4 \\
 & & & Fe=56 & Ru=104{,}_4 & Ir=198. \\
 & & & Ni=Co=59 & Pl=106{,}_6 & Os=199. \\
H=1 & & & Cu=63{,}_4 & Ag=108 & Hg=200. \\
 & Be=9{,}_4 & Mg=24 & Zn=65{,}_2 & Cd=112 \\
 & B=11 & Al=27{,}_4 & ?=68 & Ur=116 & Au=197? \\
 & C=12 & Si=28 & ?=70 & Sn=118 \\
 & N=14 & P=31 & As=75 & Sb=122 & Bi=210 \\
 & O=16 & S=32 & Se=79{,}_4 & Te=128? \\
 & F=19 & Cl=35{,}_5 & Br=80 & I=127 \\
Li=7 & Na=23 & K=39 & Rb=85{,}_4 & Cs=133 & Tl=204 \\
 & & Ca=40 & Sr=87{,}_6 & Ba=137 & Pb=207. \\
 & & ?=45 & Ce=92 \\
 & & ?Er=56 & La=94 \\
 & & ?Yt=60 & Di=95 \\
 & & ?In=75{,}_6 & Th=118? \\
\end{array}
$$

а потому приходится въ разныхъ рядахъ имѣть различное измѣненіе разностей,
чего нѣтъ въ главныхъ числахъ предлагаемой таблицы. Или же придется предпо-
лагать при составленіи системы очень много недостающихъ членовъ. То и
другое мало выгодно. Мнѣ кажется притомъ, наиболѣе естественнымъ составить
кубическую систему (предлагаемая есть плоскостная), но и попытки для ея образо-
ванія не повели къ надлежащимъ результатамъ. Слѣдующія двѣ попытки могутъ по-
казать то разнообразіе сопоставленій, какое возможно при допущеніи основнаго
начала, высказаннаго въ этой статьѣ.

Li	Na	K	Cu	Rb	Ag	Cs	—	Tl
7	23	39	63,4	85,4	108	133		204
Be	Mg	Ca	Zn	Sr	Cd	Ba	—	Pb
B	Al	—	—	—	Ur	—	—	Bi?
C	Si	Ti	—	Zr	Sn	—	—	—
N	P	V	As	Nb	Sb	—	Ta	—
O	S	—	Se	—	Te	—	W	—
F	Cl	—	Br	—	J	—	—	—
19	35,5	58	80	190	127	160	190	220.

the fourteenth elements after lithium—sodium (Na) and potassium (K)—are also reactive metals. When the elements were arranged in seven columns he noted that the first two elements in the last column (Group 7 on the table below)—fluorine (F) and chlorine (Cl)—are both reactive nonmetals.

The vertical columns on Mendeleev's table are "groups" and the horizontals are "periods." Mendeleev wrote that the elements arranged according to their atomic weight "show a periodic change of properties," and his table came to be known as the periodic table.

Mendeleev's periodic law established the following: if the elements are arranged according to their atomic weights, their properties vary in a regular and predictable way; elements with similar chemical properties have similar atomic weights, or weights separated by regular intervals; the arrangements of elements in groups corresponds to their valences (the combining power of an element expressed as the number of chemical bonds that one atom of the

element forms in a given compound) the value of the atomic weight determines an element's character.

PREDICTING THE FUTURE

One of the most noticeable features of Mendeleev's first periodic table was that, although he found room for the 63 elements known at that time, it contained a number of gaps. Mendeleev was convinced that these gaps represented elements that had not yet been discovered. He actually did much more than predict the existence of a few new elements; he also forecast, on the basis of their position in the periodic table, their atomic weights and their chemical properties. In this way, he gave detailed descriptions of three then unknown elements. These elements are now known to be scandium (Sc), gallium (Ga), and germanium (Ge).

THE NOBLE GASES

Mendeleev was unaware of one whole group on the periodic table: the group that contains the so-called "rare" gases. They are all inert—this means they are very unreactive and do not combine with other elements. Because they are so exclusive they are sometimes called the "noble" gases. The first of them, argon (Ar), was discovered in 1894 by the Scottish chemist William Ramsay (1852–1916). It had long been known that, in addition to nitrogen and oxygen,

	G1	G2	G3	G4	G5	G6	G7
Period 1	Lithium	Beryllium	Boron	Carbon	Nitrogen	Oxygen	Fluorine
Weight	7	9	11	12	14	16	19
Period 2	Sodium	Magnesium	Aluminum	Silicon	Phosphorus	Sulfur	Chlorine
Weight	23	24	27	28	31	32	35
Period 3	Potassium	Calcium		Titanium	Vanadium	Chromium	Manganese
Weight	39	40		48	51	52	55
Period 4	Rubidium	Zinc		Arsenic	Selenium	Bromine
Weight	85	65		74	78	80

ATOMIC STRUCTURE

Dalton's atomic theory, on which Mendeleev's periodic table was based, has stood the test of time. But we now know that the structure of the atom is more complex than the simple particle he envisaged.

British physicist Joseph John (J. J.) Thomson (1856–1940), who became professor of experimental physics at Cambridge University, England, in 1884, was the first person to discover that atoms have structure. This came about as a result of his investigations into the rays emitted by the cathode, the negatively charged electrode, when an electric discharge takes place in a vacuum tube. Thomson showed that the cathode "rays" are in fact tiny particles charged with negative electricity, which he named "corpuscles." We now know them as electrons.

Where had they come from? The vacuum tube was totally empty of air and contained only two metal plates: the negatively charged cathode and the positively charged anode. Because the electrons were negatively charged, their source had to be the cathode itself, and Thomson inferred that they must come from inside the atoms of the metal that formed the plate. He suggested that atoms are tiny spheres with electrons embedded in them, like blueberries in a muffin.

The next breakthrough was made in 1907 by the British physicist Ernest Rutherford (1871–1937). Alpha particles—positively charged particles given off by a radioactive element such as radium—were fired at a very thin sheet of gold foil. Most of them passed straight through. But a few of the particles came back at an angle, as if they had bounced off some obstacle in the gold foil.

Rutherford suggested that each gold atom (in fact, every kind of atom) has at its center a core called the nucleus. This has a positive charge. Most of the positively charged alpha particles were able to pass right through the gold. However, because positive charges repel (drive away) other positive charges, the particles that came near a nucleus were deflected at an angle.

Rutherford later established, in 1914, that the nucleus has a positive charge because it contains different positively charged particles called protons. His groundbreaking work showed that the atom consists of a central, positively charged nucleus containing protons, surrounded by negatively charged electrons. Each atom has an equal number of electrons and protons, but different atoms have different numbers of electrons and protons. It is these differences that account for the ordered sequence of elements in Mendeleev's periodic table.

A sketch of John Dalton, whose view of the atom as a solid particle was challenged in the 20th century by Thomson and Rutherford.

ordinary air contains a small amount of an unknown inert gas. Ramsay managed to isolate this gas and named it argon, from the Greek word meaning "lazy." He went on to discover three other gases present in air in tiny quantities: neon (Ne) "new," krypton (Kr) "hidden," and xenon (Xe) "stranger." The existence of helium (He) was first proposed by British astronomer Joseph Lockyer (1836–1920). It was confirmed by Ramsay, who isolated it in 1895. In 1900, German chemist Friedrich Dorn (1848–1916) discovered radon (Rn) in a radium sample, completing the group.

CONFIRMING MENDELEEV'S PERIODIC LAW

The discovery of the rare gases was further confirmation of Mendeleev's periodic law: they were all gases, they were all unreactive, and they could be displayed readily in a single column without conflicting with any other part of the table. The periodic law was undoubtedly his single greatest achievement. Although he had other highly practical scientific interests, such as chemical fertilizers and the petroleum industry, he was frequently in trouble for his progressive political views and his later career was marred by clashes with Russia's tsarist regime. He was removed from office in 1890, but was greatly admired and honored by the worldwide scientific community until his death in 1907. Today, Mendeleev is acknowledged for his great contribution in providing a framework for modern chemical theory.

THE IMPORTANCE OF THE ATOMIC NUMBER

Scientists now know that it is not so much the atomic weight of an element that determines its chemical properties, as Mendeleev believed, as its "atomic number." But this was something understood only after the discovery in 1897 by J. J. Thomson of the negatively charged particle, the electron. Lying somewhere in every atom is a constant number of these particles. Ernest Rutherford completed the picture when he showed that every atom has a central nucleus containing positively charged particles, or protons. The atom may be pictured as being similar to a miniature planetary system, with positive protons in its central nucleus being orbited by an equal number of negatively charged electrons. The negative charges on the electrons exactly balance the positive charges on the protons, which means that the atom carries no overall charge.

The atomic number of an element describes the number of protons in the nucleus of an atom. Hydrogen (H) is the simplest atom, with just one proton in its nucleus, which is circled by a single electron. The next atom, helium (He), has 2 protons, iron (Fe) has 26, gold (Au) 79, and so on. The more protons and electrons atoms have, the greater the weight of the atom. So whether elements are listed by their atomic weight or their atomic number, the order remains the same in the periodic table.

SCIENCE IN RUSSIA

Scientific study developed relatively late in Russia, partly because the tsarist regime was nervous about new ideas. At the start of the 19th century there were only six universities in all of Russia. Students wanting to study science often had to travel to the West to do so.

Mendeleev was probably the foremost Russian scientist of the 19th century. In more recent times major figures included the low-temperature physicist Pyotr Kapitza (1894–1984) and one of the major theoretical physicists of the 20th century, Lev Landau (1908–1968).

From 1917 to 1989 Russia was under Communist rule. Freedom of thought was

Russian cosmonaut Yuri Gagarin (1934–1968), the first human to travel in space. He orbited Earth in Vostok I in 1961.

severely restricted. Leading physicist Andrei Sakharov (1921–1989) was one of many scientists prevented from working by the authorities: he endured persecution and exile as a result of his fearless campaign for civil liberties. The influence of biologist Trofin Lysenko (1898–1977), who was favored by the regime, meant that anyone who disagreed with him would never find a job in his field.

During the Cold War (1948–89) Soviet scientists were directed to develop nuclear weapons, and to win the "space race" with the United States, which the Communists hoped would gain them international prestige. The Soviets had early successes, launching the first artificial Earth satellite in 1957, and sending the first human into space in 1961. But the effort diverted resources from other areas of science, which suffered from underdevelopment.

Moscow University was established in 1755 by Empress Elizabeth. In those days, lecturers were imported from abroad, mostly from Germany.

One further discovery proved to be significant. In 1913, Danish physicist Neils Bohr (1885–1962) put forward his model of the atom; he established that the electrons within an atom orbit the nucleus at varying distances from the nucleus; they are arranged in a series of concentric shells. This explained why elements behave in certain ways. For example, the rare or noble gases are inert (do not react with other elements) because the outermost shells of their atoms are full; they have no spare electrons to offer other elements and no empty spaces to accept another's electrons. In contrast the metals commonly known as the alkali metals—lithium (Li), sodium (Na), and potassium (K) are examples—are highly reactive because they contain just one electron in their outermost shell and will react with almost any other element to fill it. Indeed, they are so reactive that they always occur in nature combined with another element.

CREATING SYNTHETIC ELEMENTS

Chemists have continued to add new elements to the periodic table. Element 92, uranium (U), is the heaviest of the naturally occurring elements. All the elements on the periodic table after that number have been artificially created in nuclear reactors. Being radioactive, they have extremely short lives before they disintegrate ("decay") into another more stable substance.

In theory chemists should be able to create further new elements, but in practice this is not easily done. When a team of nuclear chemists made element 112 (now named copernicum) in Germany in 1998, the experiment took them 24 days, working all around the clock. At the end of this time just two atoms were created, which lasted for a few millionths of a second. In 1999, Russian and American scientists announced they had prepared a few atoms each of elements 114 (now named flerovium), 116 (livermorium), and 118 (ununoctium).

It is unlikely that many more elements will be made. This is because the higher the atomic number of an element, the greater the number of positively charged protons in the nucleus. Positive charges repel (drive away) other positive charges; the more positively charged protons there are, the greater is the force of repulsion within the nucleus. At some point—scientists are not sure when—the atomic number will be so high, and the opposing forces between the protons so great, that not even the most fleeting of nuclei will form.

SCIENTIFIC BACKGROUND

Before 1865

French chemist Antoine Lavoisier (1743–1794) lists 31 elements

English chemist John Dalton (1766–1844) founds modern atomic theory when he links the chemical properties of elements with their atomic weights

German chemist Johann Döbereiner (1780–1849) identifies "triads" of elements

1865

1865 English chemist John Newlands (1837–1898) establishes his law of octaves

1869 Mendeleev unveils his periodic table, stating that the elements arranged according to their atomic weight show a "periodic change of properties"

1870

1870 German chemist Julius Lothar Meyer (1830–1895) presents his own table of elements showing the periodic change in their properties

1870 Mendeleev completes his two-volume general textbook, *The Principles of Chemistry*

1875

1875 The first of the three elements that Mendeleev has predicted and described is discovered; it is named gallium (Ga)

1880

1879 Mendeleev's second "missing" element, scandium (Sc) is found

1885

1888 American chemist Theodore William (1868–1928) begins his quest to obtain accurate atomic weights for elements; his measurements improve on the values established by Belgian chemist Jean Stas (1813–1891)

1885 Germanium (Ge) is discovered; its properties have already been predicted by Mendeleev

1890

1895

1896 Ramsay publishes *The Gases of the Atmosphere*, in which he shows that there is an eighth group—Group 0—in the periodic table: the inert noble gases

1900

1900 German chemist Friedrich Dorn (1848–1916) discovers the final gas in Group 0: radon (Rn)

1905

After 1905

1940 American chemist Glenn Seaborg (1912–) produces the first transuranium elements (elements with an atomic number greater than that of uranium), neptunium (Np) and plutonium (Pu)

1894 The first rare or noble gas, named argon (Ar), is discovered by the Scottish chemist William Ramsay (1852–1919)

1897 The English physicist J. J. Thomson (1856–1940) discovers the electron

1999 A few atoms of elements 114 (flerovium) are produced

2002–2005 Atoms of the element 118 (ununoctium) are produced in Russian and American laboratories

POLITICAL AND CULTURAL BACKGROUND

1865

1865 Slavery is abolished in the United States

1870

1870 France declares war on Prussia, but is ill-prepared; the French emperor Napoleon III (1808–1873) is captured, and the capital, Paris, is besieged for four months

1870 The unification of Italy is completed when French troops withdraw from Rome

1875

1877 In the United States, *The Washington Post* newspaper begins publication; the first edition is four pages long

1880

1881 In Russia, Tsar Alexander II (1855–1881) is assassinated by a Polish student after failing to deliver constitutional reform

1885

1885 The first successful gasoline-driven motor car is built by German engineer Karl Benz (1844–1929)

1886 *The Strange Case of Dr Jekyll and Mr Hyde*, by Robert Louis Stevenson (1850–1894), in which a good man discovers a drug that can make him evil, is a great popular success

1888 The Suez Canal Convention is established to guarantee "free and open" access to the waterway linking the Mediterranean and the Red Sea

1890

1894 Tsar Nicholas II (1868–1917) ascends to the Russian throne; he will be overthrown and killed in the 1917 revolution

1891 Tsar Alexander III (1845–1894) of Russia approves the building of a Trans-Siberian railway; the massive project will finally be completed in 1917

1900 Russian author Anton Chekhov (1860–1904) completes one of his most celebrated plays, *Uncle Vanya*; it will be followed by *The Three Sisters* (1901) and *The Cherry Orchard* (1904)

1906 Nicholas II summons a Duma (Parliament) in order to quell widespread discontent among the Russian people; but after two months he dismisses it and imposes martial law

Key

Atomic Number — 20   40 — Atomic Weight

Ca — Chemical Symbol

Element Name — Calcium

Group	1	2	3	4	5	6	7	8	9	10	11	12	13	14	15	16	17	18
Period																		
1	1 H Hydrogen																	2 4 He Helium
2	3 7 Li Lithium	4 9 Be Beryllium											5 11 B Boron	6 12 C Carbon	7 14 N Nitrogen	8 16 O Oxygen	9 19 F Fluorine	10 20 Ne Neon
3	11 23 Na Sodium	12 24 Mg Magnesium											13 27 Al Aluminum	14 28 Si Silicon	15 31 P Phosphorus	16 32 S Sulfur	17 35 Cl Chlorine	18 40 Ar Argon
4	19 39 K Potassium	20 40 Ca Calcium	21 45 Sc Scandium	22 48 Ti Titanium	23 51 V Vanadium	24 52 Cr Chromium	25 55 Mn Manganese	26 56 Fe Iron	27 59 Co Cobalt	28 59 Ni Nickel	29 64 Cu Copper	30 65 Zn Zinc	31 70 Ga Gallium	32 73 Ge Germanium	33 75 As Arsenic	34 79 Se Selenium	35 80 Br Bromine	36 84 Kr Krypton
5	37 85 Rb Rubidium	38 88 Sr Strontium	39 89 Y Yttrium	40 91 Zr Zirconium	41 93 Nb Niobium	42 (98) Mo Molybdenum	43 101 Tc Technetium	44 103 Ru Ruthenium	45 106 Rh Rhodium	46 108 Pd Palladium	47 112 Ag Silver	48 115 Cd Cadmium	49 119 In Indium	50 122 Sn Tin	51 128 Sb Antimony	52 127 Te Tellurium	53 131 I Iodine	54 131 Xe Xenon
6	55 133 Cs Cesium	56 137 Ba Barium	57-71	72 178 Hf Hafnium	73 181 Ta Tantalum	74 184 W Tungsten	75 186 Re Rhenium	76 190 Os Osmium	77 192 Ir Iridium	78 195 Pt Platinum	79 197 Au Gold	80 201 Hg Mercury	81 204 Tl Thallium	82 207 Pb Lead	83 209 Bi Bismuth	84 (209) Po Polonium	85 (210) At Astatine	86 (222) Rn Radon
7	87 (223) Fr Francium	88 (226) Ra Radium	89-103	104 (261) Rf Rutherfordium	105 (262) Db Dubnium	106 (266) Sg Seaborgium	107 (264) Bh Bohrium	108 (277) Hs Hassium	109 (268) Mt Meitnerium	110 (281) Ds Darmstadtium	111 (280) Rg Roentgenium	112 (285) Cn Copernicium	Uut Ununtrium	Fl Flerovium	Uup Ununpentium	Lv Livermorium	Uus Ununseptium	Uuo Ununoctium

57 139 La Lanthanum	58 140 Ce Cerium	59 141 Pr Praseodymium	60 144 Nd Neodymium	61 (145) Pm Promethium	62 150 Sm Samarium	63 152 Eu Europium	64 157 Gd Gadolinium	65 159 Tb Terbium	66 163 Dy Dysprosium	67 165 Ho Holmium	68 167 Er Erbium	69 169 Tm Thulium	70 173 Yb Ytterbium	71 175 Lu Lutetium
89 (227) Ac Actinium	90 232 Th Thorium	91 231 Pa Protactinium	92 238 U Uranium	93 (237) Np Neptunium	94 (244) Pu Plutonium	95 243 Am Americium	96 (247) Cm Curium	97 (247) Bk Berkelium	98 (251) Cf Californium	99 (252) Es Einsteinium	100 (257) Fm Fermium	101 (258) Md Mendelevium	102 (259) No Nobelium	103 (262) Lr Lawrencium

Alkali Metals	Alkaline Earth Metals	Transition Elements	Other Metals	Lanthanides and Actinides	Metalloids	Other Nonmetals	Halogens	Noble Gases	Unknown

Metals   **Metalloids**   **Nonmetals**

Atomic weights in parentheses indicate elements with no standard atomic weight.

The periodic table organizes all the chemical elements into a simple chart according to the physical and chemical properties of their atoms. The elements are arranged by atomic number from 1 to 118. The atomic number is based on the number of protons in the nucleus of the atom. The atomic mass is the combined mass of protons and neutrons in the nucleus. Each element has a chemical symbol that is an abbreviation of its name. In some cases, such as potassium, the symbol is an abbreviation of its Latin name ("K" stands for *kalium*). The name by which the element is commonly known is given in full underneath the symbol. The last item in the element box is the atomic mass. This is the average mass of an atom of the element.

Scientists have arranged the elements into vertical columns called groups and horizontal rows called periods. Elements in any one group all have the same number of electrons in their outer shell and have similar chemical properties. Periods represent the increasing number of electrons it takes to fill the inner and outer shells and become stable. When all the spaces have been filled (Group 18 atoms have all their shells filled) the next period begins.

acid Substance that dissolves in water to form hydrogen ions (H+). Acids are neutralized by alkalis and have a pH below 7.

actinides Metals that with the lanthanides form the elements commonly referred to as the rare-earth metals. All actinide metals are radioactive.

alchemist Person who attempts to change one substance into another using a combination of primitive chemistry and magic.

alkali Substance that dissolves in water to form hydroxide ions (OH–). Alkalis have a pH greater than 7 and will react with acids to form salts.

alkali metals Those metals that form Group 1 of the periodic table.

alkaline-earth metals Those metals that form Group 2 of the periodic table.

allotrope A different form of an element in which the atoms are arranged in a different structure.

alloy A metallic substance that contains two or more metals. An alloy may also be made of a metal and a small amount of a nonmetal. Steel, for example, is an alloy of iron and carbon.

amalgam Alloys that are made with mercury.

atom The smallest independent building block of matter. All substances are made of atoms.

atomic mass number The total number of protons and neutrons in an atom's nucleus.

atomic number The number of protons in a nucleus.

base A substance that produces hydroxide ions (OH–).

boiling point The temperature at which a liquid turns into a gas.

bond The chemical connection between atoms.

brass An alloy of copper and zinc.

bronze An alloy made of copper and tin.

chemical equation Symbols and numbers that show how reactants change into products during a chemical reaction.

chemical formula The letters and numbers that represent a chemical compound, such as "H2O" for water.

chemical reaction The reaction of two or more chemicals (the reactants) to form new chemicals (the products).

chemical symbol The letters that represent a chemical, such as "Cl" for chlorine or "Na" for sodium.

combustion The reaction that causes burning. Combustion is generally a reaction with oxygen in the air.

compound Substance made from more than one element and that has undergone a chemical reaction.

conductor A substance that carries electricity and heat well.

covalent bond Bond in which atoms share one or more electrons.

crystal A solid made of regular repeating patterns of atoms.

crystal lattice The regular repeated structure found in crystalline solids.

diatomic molecule Compound in which two nonmetal atoms, whether the same or different elements, are joined by the attraction of sharing electrons (covalent bonds).

dissolve To form a solution.

ductile Describes materials that can be stretched into a thin wire. Many metals are ductile.

elastic Describes a substance that returns to its original shape after being stretched.

electricity A stream of electrons or other charged particles moving through a substance.

electrolysis A method of separating elements in ionic compounds by dissolving the compound in an appropriate solvent and passing an electric current through the solution.

electromagnetic radiation The energy emitted by a source in the form of gamma rays, X-rays, ultraviolet light, visible light, infrared, microwaves, or radio waves.

electromagnetic spectrum The range of energy waves that includes light, heat, and radio waves.

electron A tiny negatively charged particle that moves around the nucleus of an atom.

element A material that cannot be broken up into simpler ingredients. Elements contain only one type of atom.

energy level Electron shells around an atom represent different energy levels. Those closest to the nucleus have the lowest energy.

fission Process by which a large atom breaks up into two or more smaller fragments.

four elements The ancient theory that all matter consisted of only four elements (earth, air, fire, and water) and their combinations.

fusion When small atoms fuse to make a single larger atom.

gas State in which particles are not joined and are free to move in any direction.

group A column of related elements in the periodic table.

halogens Mainly gaseous nonmetals belonging to Group 17 of the periodic table.

ion An atom that has lost or gained one or more electrons.

ionic bond Bond in which one atom gives one or more electrons to another atom.

isotope Atoms of a given element must have the same number of protons but can have different numbers of neutrons. These different versions of the same element are called isotopes.

lanthanides Metals that, with the actinides, form the elements commonly referred to as the rare-earth metals.

liquid Substance in which particles are loosely bonded and are able to move freely around each other.

malleable Describes a material that can be hammered into different shapes without breaking. Metals are malleable.

melting point The temperature at which a solid changes into a liquid. When a liquid changes into a solid, this same temperature is called the freezing point.

metal An element that is solid, shiny, malleable, ductile, and conductive.

metalloid Elements that have properties of both metals and nonmetals.

mineral A natural compound that occurs in rocks and soil.

molecule Two or more joined atoms that have a unique shape and size.

neutron One of the particles that make up the nucleus of an atom. Neutrons do not have any electric charge.

noble gases A group of gases that rarely react with other elements because they have a full outer shell of electrons.

nonmetal Any element that is not a metal. Most nonmetals are gases, such as hydrogen and argon. These elements are grouped on the right-hand side of the periodic table.

nucleus The central part of an atom. The nucleus contains protons and neutrons. The exception is hydrogen, which contains only one proton.

ore A mineral that contains valuable amounts of materials such as copper, sulfur, or tin.

period A row of elements across the periodic table.

phase change A change from one state to another.

pressure The force produced by pressing on something.

proton A positively charged particle found in an atom's nucleus.

radiation The products of radioactivity—alpha and beta particles and gamma rays.

radioactive decay The breakdown of an unstable nucleus through the loss of alpha and beta particles.

rare-earth metals Metals that form two rows of elements—the actinides and the lanthanides—below the main body of the periodic table.

reactivity The tendency of an element to react chemically with other elements.

salt An ionic compound made by reacting an acid with an alkali.

semiconductor A substance that conducts heat and electricity but only in certain circumstances.

shell The orbit of an electron. Each shell can contain a specific number of electrons and no more.

solid State of matter in which particles are held in a rigid arrangement.

solution A mixture of two or more elements or compounds in a single phase (solid, liquid, or gas).

standard conditions Normal room temperature and pressure.

state The form that matter takes—either a solid, a liquid, or a gas.

steel An alloy of iron and carbon.

temperature A measure of how fast molecules are moving.

thiols Compounds of sulfur that often have strong or unpleasant smells.

transition metals Those metals that make up groups 3 through 12 of the periodic table.

transuranium elements Elements with an atomic number greater than that of uranium, which is 92.

valence A measure of the number of bonds an atom can form with other atoms.

valence electrons The electrons in the outer shell of an atom.

volume The space that a solid, liquid, or gas occupies.

wavelength The distance measured from the peak of one wave to the peak of the next wave.

American Association for the
Advancement of Science (AAAS)
1200 New York Avenue NW
Washington, DC 20005
(202) 326-6400
Web site: http://www.aaas.org
Founded in 1848, AAAS serves some 261
affiliated societies and academies of
science and publishes the peer-
reviewed general science journal
Science. The non-profit AAAS is open
to all and fulfills its mission to advance
science and serve society through ini-
tiatives that include science policy,
international programs, science
education.

American Chemical Society (ACS)
1155 Sixteenth Street NW
Washington, DC 20036
(800) 227-5558
Web site: http://www.acs.org/content/
acs/en.html
With more than 163,000 members, the
American Chemical Society (ACS)
is the world's largest scientific
society and one of the world's leading sources of authoritative
scientific information. A nonprofit
organization, chartered by
Congress, ACS is at the forefront of
the evolving worldwide chemical
enterprise and the premier profes-
sional home for chemists, chemical
engineers, and related professions
around the globe. ACS is commit-
ted to improving people's lives
through the transforming power of
chemistry.

Brookhaven National Laboratory
Chemistry Department, Bldg. 555A
P.O. Box 5000
Upton, NY 11973-5000
(631) 344-4301
Web site: http://www.bnl.gov/chemistry/
default.asp
The Chemistry Department of the
Brookhaven National Laboratory conducts basic research in the chemical
sciences on subjects ranging from
nuclear processes shortly after the big
bang to medical imaging, and many
topics in between. Major topics of the
department's research includes: cataly-
sis and surface science; charge transfer
for energy conversion; chemistry with
ionizing radiation; nanoscience; combustion; nuclear chemistry; and
experimental and theoretical programs
studying imaging and neuroscience.

Journal of Biological Chemistry
c/o ASBMB
11200 Rockville Pike, Suite 302
Rockville, MD 20852-3110
(240) 283-6620
Web site: http://www.jbc.org
The Journal of Biological Chemistry publishes papers based on original
research that are judged to make a
novel and important contribution to
understanding the molecular and cel-
lular basis of biological processes.

The National Science Foundation
Division of Chemistry
4201 Wilson Boulevard
Arlington, VA 22230

(703) 292-5111

Web site: http://www.nsf.gov/div/index.jsp?div=CHE

The mission of the Division of Chemistry is to promote the health of academic chemistry and to enable basic research and education in the chemical sciences. The division also supports projects that help build infrastructure, workforce, and partnerships that advance the chemical sciences.

The Nobel Prize in Chemistry
Nobel Media AB
Sturegatan 14
Box 5232
SE-102 45 Stockholm
Sweden
Tel.: +46 8 663 17 22
Web site: http://www.nobelprize.org/nobel_prizes/chemistry/

The Chemistry Prize has been awarded to 163 Nobel Laureates since 1901. Chemistry was the most important science for Alfred Nobel's own work. The development of his inventions as well as the industrial processes he employed were based upon chemical knowledge. Chemistry was the second prize area that Nobel mentioned in his will. The Nobel Prize in Chemistry is awarded by the Royal Swedish Academy of Sciences, Stockholm, Sweden.

Royal Society of Chemistry (RSC)
Burlington House
Piccadilly, London W1J 0BA
England

Tel.: +44 (0)20 7437 8656
Web site: http://www.rsc.org

The RSC is the largest organization in Europe for advancing the chemical sciences. Supported by a worldwide network of members and an international publishing business, its activities span education, conferences, science policy, and the promotion of chemistry to the public.

Science Magazine
1200 New York Avenue NW
Washington, DC 20005
(202) 326-6550
Web site: http://www.sciencemag.org

Founded in 1880 on $10,000 of seed money from the American inventor Thomas Edison, *Science* has grown to become the world's leading outlet for scientific news, commentary, and cutting-edge research, with the largest paid circulation of any peer-reviewed general-science journal. Through its print and online incarnations, *Science* reaches an estimated worldwide readership of more than one million. Its articles consistently rank among world's most cited research.

WEB SITES

Due to the changing nature of Internet links, Rosen Publishing has developed an online list of Web sites related to the subject of this book. This site is updated regularly. Please use this link to access the list:

http://www.rosenlinks.com/CORE/Per

Brown, Theodore E., et al. *Chemistry: The Central Science*. Upper Saddle River, NJ: Prentice Hall, 2011.

Chang, Raymond, and Kenneth A. Goldsby. *Chemistry*. New York, NY: McGraw-Hill Science/Engineering/Math, 2012.

Curran, Greg. *Homework Helpers: Chemistry*. Pompton Plains, NJ: Career Press, 2011.

Gilbert, Thomas R. *Chemistry: The Science in Context*. New York, NY: W.W. Norton & Co., 2011.

Gray, Theodore. *The Elements: A Visual Exploration of Every Known Atom in the Universe*. New York, NY: Black Dog & Leventhal Publishers, 2012.

Gray, Theodore. *The Photographic Card Deck of the Elements: With Big Beautiful Photographs of All 118 Elements in the Periodic Table*. New York, NY: Black Dog & Leventhal Publishers, 2010.

Gray, Theodore, and Simon Quellen Field. *Theodore Gray's Elements Vault: Treasures of the Periodic Table with Removable Archival Documents and Real Element Samples—Including Pure Gold!* New York, NY: Black Dog & Leventhal Publishers, 2011.

Jackson, Tom. *The Elements: An Illustrated History of the Periodic Table*. New York, NY: Shelter Harbor Press, 2012.

Kean, Sam. *The Disappearing Spoon: And Other True Tales of Madness, Love, and the History of the World from the Periodic Table of the Elements*. New York, NY: Back Bay Books, 2011.

Mikulecky, Peter J., et al. *Chemistry Workbook for Dummies*. Hoboken, NJ: Wiley Publishing, 2008.

Moore, John T. *Chemistry for Dummies*. Hoboken, NJ: For Dummies, 2011.

Silberberg, Martin. *Chemistry: The Molecular Nature of Matter and Change*. New York, NY: McGraw-Hill Science/Engineering/Math, 2011.

Timberlake, Karen C. *Chemistry: An Introduction to General, Organic, and Biological Chemistry*. Upper Saddle River, NJ: Prentice Hall, 2011.

PHOTO CREDITS